The Elementary Teacher's Guide to Conferences & Open Houses

Grades K-5

by

Melissa Hughes

Kristin Oakes

Caroline Lenzo

Jackie Carpas

Table of Contents

Introduction

About This Book...

Conferences and open houses are too often the only opportunities you have to build an effective partnership with the parents of your students. Therefore, a great deal is riding on your ability to put your best foot forward. Being well-prepared for a conference or open house is the best strategy for making the most of the time you have with parents. **That is the goal of this book: to provide you with everything you need to make all types of conferences easier and more productive for you, your students, and their parents.**

How to hold traditional conferences between parents and teachers is thoroughly covered here, but this book goes a step further by including step-by-step instructions about how to hold alternative conferences and open houses. You will learn how to involve students in creative ways of sharing their own academic strengths and weaknesses with their parents. **This book includes ready-to-use sample conference and open house invitations, parent surveys, and evaluation forms. You will also find a handy reference list of ways to communicate student progress and a list of dos and don'ts for conferences.**

Whether you are planning a large, elaborate open house or a small conference with just one parent, this book will guide you through using conferences and open houses to build this important partnership between home and school. Don't be surprised if you find that you begin to look forward to conferences as opportunities for you and your students to share with parents the work and progress that you and their child have made. Good luck!

What's So Bad about Conferences and Open Houses?

Let's face it—parents often feel that when they are asked to come to school for a conference, there must be a problem. Personal conferences are certainly effective and beneficial ways to discuss problems, indicate areas in need of improvement, and offer strategies for success, but they still have that negative stigma attached. By working with students and school personnel to change negative perceptions of conferences, both you and parents will feel more relaxed, and conferences will be far more productive and will have less potential for being confrontational.

The best way to prevent conferences from being stressful is to provide many additional opportunities for parents to come to school, meet you, and see your students working in the learning environment you have created for them. Help parents learn to feel comfortable about visiting school. Demonstrate your teaching style and show how their children are part of your classroom's learning community by inviting them to be a guest reader, share careers or hobbies, serve as a party helper, or be a lunch or trip volunteer.

Likewise, regular communication between home and school is a powerful tool for keeping parents informed about what is happening in your classroom and making sure there are no surprises. Accomplish this on a regular basis by frequently sending updates and sharing good news through newsletters, postcards, a take-home classroom publication, or e-mails; writing comments on progress reports; awarding achievement certificates; or even adding stickers and comments to graded papers.

General Conference/Open House Guidelines

Getting ready for conferences and open houses takes time, but you will save yourself time afterward by being prepared before the event. And, parents will be impressed with the effort you made!

Planning a conference or open house is like planning a party. Make yourself a checklist or use the **Facilitation Checklist: Present Yourself as a Professional!** *(page 25) to make remembering all of the necessary information easier.*

Getting Ready to Meet

Getting ready to meet one parent or a group of parents can seem overwhelming, but there are ways to make less work for yourself. For all conferences and open houses, especially the first one, you will make a good impression by being prepared and organized. Being prepared reduces your anxiety and maximizes your meeting time by allowing you to focus on sharing information about your students.

When preparing for your conferences and open houses, regardless of whether they are traditional or alternative, there are certain steps that will ensure you have not forgotten anything, and that you, your students, and their parents are ready. This chapter is devoted to getting you ready for any type of meeting with parents. You will find helpful hints for:

- setting a purpose (pages 4-5)
- establishing a format (pages 5-6)
- surveying parents (page 6)
- scheduling (page 9)
- arranging a waiting area (page 10)
- preparing your classroom (pages 10-11)
- gathering materials and forms (pages 11-12)
- documenting a conference (pages 12-13)
- evaluating the experience (pages 13-14)
- filing and tracking paperwork (page 14)
- following up (page 14)
- handling a difficult conference (pages 15-16)
- confidentiality (page 17)

In addition, this book is full of reproducible checklists and forms which make preparation, scheduling, conferencing, and documentation more convenient (see page 18 for this chapter's work sheet overview).

☑ Setting a purpose for your conferences/open houses

Teachers have conferences and open houses for many reasons. One reason is that most schools have scheduled conference and open house periods. Another reason is that an occasion has arisen (usually a behavioral concern or a question about academic performance or placement) where parents must be consulted. A third, important reason should be to share information about classroom activities or the learning environment. Holding conferences and open houses for the third reason can help you build supportive relationships with parents.

General Conference/Open House Guidelines

Whether you are planning for your school's scheduled conferences, open house, or other specific meeting, you should establish a main purpose for each individual conference. Think about the different ways you could prepare for each of these meetings:

- discussing a change in academic performance or subject placement
- establishing a communication plan for assignments and homework
- discussing learning strategies and extra help available
- developing motivational strategies to improve attitude
- sharing testing information
- setting up Individual Education Plans (IEPs) (see pages 35-36)
- informing parents of any change in behavior
- sharing report card information
- discussing the possibility of retention or of skipping a grade
- sharing plans for providing more challenging material
- meeting with an Intervention Assistance Team to assist with behavior modification
- holding a subject area conference
- educating parents about their child's new school and classroom
- having a family night (see page 88)
- showcasing work or projects
- teaching parents about upcoming testing

Early in the year, it is important to meet with as many parents as possible, and begin on a positive note. If a child begins a downward slide behaviorally or academically later in the year, you will not be as anxious about contacting the parent. You will have already made the parent your partner, and you can both get to work on solving the problem.

☑ Establishing a Format

Your preparation for each of the meetings listed above will be different. In order to establish the format of your conferences and open houses, you need to determine how best to present the information you have to offer. This may happen simultaneously with the next step, *Surveying Parents* (see page 6). Consider questions such as: *Are you in a self-contained classroom? If not, will you allow parents to meet with several teachers at once? Did you ask for the conference, or did a parent request it? Will the student be present* (see pages 32-33)? The answer to each question may differ from child to child, and this will help to shape the format.

For example, if you plan to include students in your conferences and use an alternative, student-led format, you will need to allot class time to coach students and tell them what to expect. If you are planning a conference around the difficult topic of grade retention, you will probably not want the student present, and you may not want to schedule any other conferences during that after-school period, due to the stressful nature of the topic. If you plan to videotape an open house, then you will need to plan the events which will be videotaped, get equipment from the library, etc.

Next, consider what style you are most comfortable with. Just as teachers have different teaching styles, they also have different styles of holding meetings. If you are introverted, you may wish to avoid large group meetings, and instead schedule student-led conferences and let your students do a lot of the talking. If you like to host parties, then do it—in the form of an open house or content conference. Although some topics (or the rules your school has for meeting) may require you to follow a certain format, don't hesitate to branch out and try a new format. Make sure to read the sections in this book which compare and contrast traditional and alternative conferences and open houses (pages 7-8), to get an idea of what each type of conference or open house will entail, and what format will best fit each situation.

Many children of divorced parents (or even parents who hyphenate) have last names which are different from those of one or both parents. Be sure to note this prior to conference time to avoid confusion.

☑ SURVEYING PARENTS

An essential step to establishing your format is finding out what parents want to know. If you know ahead of time what parents would like to cover, you can better estimate how much time you need. You can also determine whether a traditional or alternative conference or open house is more appropriate to convey the information parents need. For example, Joel's parents may need to talk to you about a private matter, while Jeanetta's, Darren's, and Suki's parents want to know how much their children's reading has improved. With this information, you might decide to have a Language Arts Content Conference for the class and schedule an additional, private conference for Joel's parents. To find out what parents want to learn, send home the following surveys and ask that they be returned at least a week before your first conference, so that you have adequate time to prepare.

- **Pre-Conference/Open House Parent Survey** (page 19)
- **Pre-Conference/Open House Student Survey** (page 20)
- **Beginning-of-the-Year Open House Parent Survey** (page 77)
- **Beginning-of-the-Year Open House Student Survey** (page 78)

Helping parents prepare for the conference or open house is as important as surveying them. If parents do not know what to expect, they have a greater chance of feeling disappointed. Suggest that they keep a copy of their answers to the survey, and encourage them to:

- bring a list of topics to share
- write down additional questions in advance
- ask their children if they have questions for the teacher

Finally, consider involving the students in the survey process. They may have questions too, and if they will be actively involved in facilitating the conference, they should also be involved in the survey!

Types of Conferences and Open Houses Defined

Once you have surveyed parents and students and considered upcoming events, you can more easily decide on a format for your conference or open house. Keep in mind that even if you choose a group format, some parents may still wish to meet with you individually. Read ahead for descriptions of the different types of conferences and open houses.

☑ Traditional conferences defined

The common definition of a traditional conference is a formal, teacher-directed meeting between parent and teacher. The format can be altered slightly if other teachers or administrators are included, or if the student is allowed to attend (but not facilitate) part of the conference. The purpose is generally to inform parents of student progress, strengths, and/or weaknesses in both academic and behavioral areas.

Traditional Conference Pros
- private
- structured
- parent/teacher collaboration

Traditional Conference Cons
- little or no input from student
- anxiety from parents
- if prescheduled by school, allows little time to meet

Traditional conferences are what schools usually have in mind when they schedule conference days. For this reason, there may be only a small increment of time available for each parent. However, they are private and intensive, and usually provide an opportunity to convey a lot of information at once. Any conference in which confidential or sensitive information is to be shared should take place in this format.

☑ Alternative conferences defined

An alternative conference is any type of parent/teacher/student meeting which does not fit the criteria listed for traditional conferences (see above). These can be student-directed within the parent-teacher format, with the student acting as facilitator and sharing his or her progress and goals. It can also mean holding a content conference, which is also student-facilitated, and involves rotating parents and students through stations in the classroom to show work and skills.

Alternative Conference Pros
- students become self-aware
- relaxed atmosphere
- parent/teacher/student
- parents hear about student directly from the student

Alternative Conference Cons
- cannot hold private discussion (applies to content conference)
- involves more student preparation
- little individual contact with parents (applies to content conference)

☑ Traditional open houses defined

Traditional open houses usually, although not always, happen at the beginning of the year. Unlike conferences, open houses are designed for groups; parents are not expected to address concerns about their children. The purpose of having a traditional open house is to give parents and students a chance to become familiar with school, teachers, classrooms, class schedules, and possibly classmates. This may be the first time students and parents see your classroom. Creating an inviting atmosphere and giving students something to look forward to can help start your year on a positive note.

Traditional Open House Pros

- able to see many families in a short time
- helps students overcome first day of school anxiety
- parents and students are not on the spot

Traditional Open House Cons

- no private time for discussions
- emphasis on first impressions
- can seem rushed

☑ Alternative open houses defined

Even if it isn't the beginning of the year, there are many reasons a school or an individual teacher may want to hold an open house. Some schools and teachers may prefer to have an open house after students are familiar with the environment, rather than at the beginning of the school year. Also, there may be events, such as plays, student art exhibits, or the advent of standardized testing, that require inviting a large group of parents to school. Because these types of open houses do not involve individual student concerns, they are listed under the alternative open house/parent meeting category.

Alternative Open House Pros

- able to see many families in a short time
- forum to explain, display, and reinforce many different policies and procedures
- relaxed atmosphere
- flexible

Alternative Open House Cons

- no private time for discussions
- requires a lot of time for preparation
- parents may be hesitant to participate

Scheduling

Scheduling conferences and open houses can be challenging. Larger class sizes mean more conferences to schedule, and more people to accommodate. Also, there are many working, single, or divorced parents who may prefer to meet with you separately in order to focus on the child rather than on familial conflict. Additionally, if children have more than one teacher, you may have to coordinate your conference with other teachers.

For any conference in which students will actively participate, it never hurts to do a "dry run" of the conference ahead of time. Students will be more focused and more comfortable if they know what to expect before the big day.

☑ Invitations

After you have set a purpose and format, give parents and students a general idea of what to expect, especially if the conference or open house is not a regular meeting as prescribed by the school calendar. Send a **General Conference/Open House Invitation** (page 21), letter, or e-mail, or make a brief phone call to outline the purpose of the conference. Offer choices between several dates and times. Briefly identify what you plan to discuss so that parents can prepare. Also, remember that if your students are to facilitate the conference, you will need to devote class time to helping them know what to expect.

☑ Make a schedule and stick to it!

Because of parents' varied schedules, you can no longer assume that parents' needs can be met during the school's typical conference times. You will need to accommodate all parents, so plan to have some meetings that are not during regular school hours. You may realize that, especially if you plan to hold your conferences or open houses during a school-scheduled conference period, it may be very difficult to fit everyone in and still remain on schedule! However, if you are having individual conferences with a number of parents, it is imperative that you stick to the schedule you have made. Follow these guidelines to help yourself stick to the schedule:

- Allot extra time in each conference or open house for questions.
- Send out **General Conference/Open House Reminders** (page 22) with instructions for how to reschedule.
- As you receive confirmations, fill out a **General Conference/Open House Scheduling Form** (page 23.) Use one for each day of conferences. Post them in your waiting area and in the classroom.
- Provide a copy of the schedule to the school office in case parents need to call and confirm or cancel.
- Encourage waiting parents to knock if a conference runs over its allotted time.
- Set a timer (non-ticking) as you begin the conference.
- Reschedule time to talk with parents and students if the conference runs over five minutes late.

Post the **General Conference/Open House Scheduling Form** *(page 23) in your waiting area. Copy it on brightly colored or neon paper to help parents spot it and keep up with their own schedules. Make sure you also have a copy in the classroom so that you can keep track of time and who is next to see you.*

Preparing Your Classroom and Materials

Regardless of what type of conference or open house you are planning, you will need to get your room and waiting area ready for parents and students. Try to think of this as a party. Your conference attendees are your guests, and part of your job is to make them feel welcome and comfortable. Likewise, anyone who is helping you facilitate the conference, including students and other teachers, is a cohost. So, use the following tips to make sure your room and waiting area are ready, and your cohosts are prepared for their roles.

Don't forget that the hallway near your classroom may be where parents wait for conferences. Get help updating bulletin boards and other hallway displays if necessary.

☑ A warm waiting area

Wait time before a conference should be a time to explore! Make sure that the waiting room (or if necessary, the hallway) is as inviting as possible. Look around. Are the bulletin boards decorated and up-to-date? Is your classroom door clearly marked with your name and grade level? Are all of the lightbulbs working, or should you put in a maintenance request to have some replaced? The waiting area will be the first impression parents get.

A waiting area is a good place to put fun projects like poems, artwork, class books, etc. If you have the space, consider providing light refreshments for waiting parents. Also, don't forget to post a copy of your schedule, hang a sign that says, "Please knock when it is time for your conference!" and provide a clock that has been synchronized with the clock or timer inside the classroom.

☑ A classroom with class

Even if you do not have a state-of-the-art school building, you can take a few simple steps to show parents that your learning environment is as bright as your students. For starters, provide adult chairs for your parents. If this is not possible, sit with them in student chairs. Having everyone sitting on the same level is an important body-language signal. For the same reason, a round or square meeting table is preferable to a rectangular table, because no one is at the head or the foot.

Keep some basic supplies handy, such as tissues (yes, sometimes parents cry at conferences), a stack of textbooks, pens and paper, and air freshener. These will help your room feel more homey and less institutional, and parents feel more comfortable putting their children into a homelike atmosphere.

Finally, remember that even if they are not attending them, your students can help you prepare for any sort of conference, and will be excited to tell their parents they made a difference. Have a class cleaning day and let all students spend a half hour at the end of the day cleaning tables and chalkboards, straightening bookshelves, clearing their desks of unwanted clutter, and attaching name tags so that their parents can see where they sit. Decorate bulletin boards with student work and art (make sure to include a few pieces from each student so no one is left out), as well as photographs of each child working in class. Display a large welcome poster and let all the students sign it.

Allowing students to help you clean up before conferences has added benefits. Students will be excited about the break from the routine, and will probably tell their parents—taking a little of that excitement home!

If your conference or open house includes the use of stations, set them up near the end of the day of the conference. Assign a small group of students to each station, telling them to make a list of everything they find at the station. Check their lists against the checklist you have already made. If they do not match, double-check that station! Also, be sure that any electrical equipment you plan to use, such as a VCR or tape recorder, is working and that all of the tapes you want to use are rewound to the correct place.

☑ Gathering materials

Before discussing academics, put together a portfolio of the child's work samples that support your concerns (see page 42 for more information on portfolios).

Remember to gather needed class work and textbooks, and to list the topics you will be discussing and any comments you have on a **Conference Summary Form** (page 24).

Before discussing behavior, check the child's records for documentation of the behavior, as well as any previous plans and contracts established to deal with the behavior. Also, ask other teachers who work with the child if they have observed the same behavior. Look for additional help and support from the counselor or principal. Some school districts offer Intervention Assistance Teams (IATs) which can help to identify the problems and formulate intervention strategies.

☑ **Student stacks**

Nothing is more distracting to parents than a teacher who shuffles through paper. Save yourself from disorganization by making a "pile" for each student. Since concrete grade information is helpful in identifying averages and progress, assemble the following for each student:

- work and homework samples from each subject
- previous conference notes
- attendance records
- report cards
- behavioral notes

Use your filled-in **Conference/Open House Scheduling Form** (page 23) as a guide so that you do not waste time trying to find what you need. Then, in each student's stack, arrange the samples in the same order as the subjects you teach. For example, if you teach math first and science second, put math samples on top and science next.

☑ **Finalizing forms**

Get ready to answer individual questions from parents by making sure that all of your forms, such as the **Pre-Conference/Open House Surveys** (pages 19-20), your own notes, progress reports, etc., and a **Conference Summary Form** (page 24), are pre-programmed with topics for the child. Place each child's forms on top of his or her work sample stack. Finally, rubber band or clip each child's samples together. At the end of each conference, you can restack everything and rubber band the work together to return to the child or send home with parents.

If you are nervous or are new to conferencing, give the ***Facilitation Checklist*** *(page 25) to a trusted friend or colleague and hold a practice conference. Have a friend or colleague mark the areas which need improvement.*

During a Conference or Open House

Keep in mind that you are the facilitator of every conference you give, and it is your job to set the pace and the tone. Parents and students will look to you for cues about how to act during a conference. Use the **Facilitation Checklist: Present Yourself as a Professional!** (page 25) as a reminder to present yourself professionally during any conference situation, and be sure to read the sections on the different types of conferences and open houses for more specific facilitating tips.

☑ **Documenting a conference**

Unfortunately, people (including teachers and parents) have imperfect memories. Many teachers have found that after a period of time has passed, they discover that they and parents of a student had set completely different expectations resulting from a conference. Keeping good records during the conference ensures that you and the parents have something to refer to after the conference is over, in case there are any gaps between your understandings.

The **Conference Summary Form** (page 24), a tool for recording information during conversations, actually saves time prior to the conference because you can check off the concerns you and parents have before the conference begins. A summary of the conference and the agreed-upon strategies can be filled in during the conference. At the end of each conference, both you and the parents should sign the summary form, and each of you should keep a copy for your records. Close the conference by summarizing what was discussed and documenting the important points on the form. Have parents sign the form and any other paperwork, and provide them with a copy. This way, documentation is complete by the end of a conference. Date each conference summary, and note each time you make contact with the parents, or have fulfilled your responsibilities with any academic or behavioral plan which was implemented for the child.

To avoid the interruption of copying during a conference, have the ***Conference Summary Form*** *(page 24) preprinted on pressure-sensitized paper, or use carbon paper as you write. Then, you have copies at your fingertips!*

You can also use the Conference Summary Form for telephone conferences (see page 33) to help you organize your thoughts and document the parent contact and agreed-upon strategies. Send a copy of this form to parents.

After a Conference or Open House

The conference/open house process does not end when the students and parents go home. Organization and evaluation of the meeting are just as important. Read the following suggestions for record keeping, continued parent communication, and evaluation.

☑ Evaluating the Experience

You will be full of questions at the end of your conference sessions. How did the conferences go? Did you meet your purpose? Were you comfortable with the format? Were you able to address all the issues you were hoping to? How could you improve your conferences? What should you definitely do again? What should you never, ever do again? Before you close the door on your conferences, no matter how busy your schedule, take some time to reflect on each of these questions, and make a few notes for next time. You need to self-evaluate while the event is still fresh in your mind, and you will only save yourself time in the long run. Use the **Teacher Conference/Open House Reflection Form** (page 26) to be honest with yourself. Pat yourself on the back where you can, and think about (and jot down) what you would like to change next time.

Also, don't hesitate to ask parents to share their ideas and feedback with you. Providing a **Conference/Open House Evaluation Form** (page 39) or **Beginning-of-the-Year Open House Evaluation Form** (page 83) is an easy way to gain feedback and improve your conferencing skills. The information you will get from these forms can provide you with insightful feedback from both the parents and the students following the conference, as well as provide further opportunities for parents to identify concerns or questions that were not addressed in the conference. For best results, hand them out at the end of each conference, then save them in a sealed envelope. Only after you have filled out one for yourself should you read the forms from parents, so that you can compare your impressions of the conferences to theirs.

Finally, your students can offer surprisingly accurate and helpful insight, especially if they were present during the conference. The next day in class, congratulate your students on their participation. Discuss with them how they perceived the night went. Be sure to let them know what they did well and how proud you are of them. It was, after all, a combined effort to share student progress with parents.

☑ Filing and Tracking

Each school district has a different policy for filing conference forms. Whether you are required to file conference summaries in the child's permanent records or file them in your classroom, keep records organized so that you and other teachers can refer to them as needed. Conference summaries can provide you with the documentation of interventions tried and signed agreements. They also document a child's behavior pattern over the years.

☑ Following Up

Use the **Conference Summary Form** (page 24) to monitor any agreements you made with parents. Formal agreements will have contracts, but there may be informal actions that you will have to remind yourself to follow up on, such as calling on a student more frequently, giving a student extra work if he or she finishes early, etc. You may even need an additional schedule to set follow-up date goals for yourself, so that parents feel you have responded to them in a timely fashion, and so that you can monitor whether goals are being reached.

Special Considerations for Conferences

When conducting a conference, sensitive issues may arise that require you to be diplomatic and professional. The following information discusses how a teacher can deal with difficult issues, defensive parents, and confidentiality.

☑ Handling a difficult conference

The emphasis of this book is on making parent encounters positive experiences. Although the vast majority of parents you meet will be cooperative and supportive, at some time in your career you will probably either anticipate a conference with a difficult parent, or get caught up in one with little or no warning. A confrontational conference can be one of the most unpleasant experiences a teacher faces, but forming a plan before it happens can help you handle it well.

First, consider what it is like to be a parent who is not also a teacher. Too often the only time parents hear from their child's school is when there is a problem. After a few such experiences, they think, "Now what's the matter?" when they receive a conference notice. They can be anxious, embarrassed, angry, or defensive. Often, parents of children with problems don't know what to do to improve a situation, and feel that you expect them to have an answer. This may lead them to skip the conference, which in turn angers and disappoints you because you worked hard to prepare.

Remember that feeling you or a classmate may have had when called to the principal's office? That feeling doesn't change if you are being called in to talk about problems with your child!

Of course, most parents do show up for conferences, but regardless of your good intentions and preparation, sometimes a parent may have built up so much anxiety or anger prior to the meeting that the conference dissolves and the parent's anger takes over. A parent may become abusive, loud, or profane. In the face of a parent's anger, it may be difficult to maintain your composure, but strive to stay calm and avoid arguing with the parent and escalating the situation. You may feel "right," but arguing with the parent makes you wrong because you are not acting as a professional. Be sure to consult the **Handling a Difficult Conference Checklist** (page 27) to find ways to diffuse the parent's anger, as well as your own!

Don't hesitate to ask another colleague, such as another teacher or the principal, to sit in on any conference with you, especially if it promises to be a difficult one. Sometimes having others present helps to keep the discussion focused on the child.

Having a form nearby to take notes during a difficult conference serves more purposes than just documentation. It also gives you something to keep yourself focused on the problems being discussed, and will make the parent feel his or her concerns are being listened to and recorded. It's hard to yell at someone who is writing down everything you say!

Preparation is still the most important tool you have against shouting matches. As with any other conference, gather work samples and written notes about anecdotal examples, and fill out the **Conference Summary Form** (page 24). Make sure that you have documentation to back up anything you are going to say. Above all, do not let a parent "drop in" and pressure (ambush!) you into an impromptu conference. These types of meetings are more likely to leave you and the parent angry and frustrated because you will not be prepared to answer all of the questions the parent has. If a parent does drop in unexpectedly and the conversation begins to turn sour, immediately stop the conversation and suggest the two of you choose another time to meet.

☑ Documenting a difficult conference

If possible, prior to the conference, state your concerns in a nonthreatening manner on the **Conference Summary Form** (page 24). Remember to document important details and information shared throughout the conference. Set goals together, and once participants agree to their responsibilities, put it in writing, complete with signatures.

Even if you and parents do not see eye-to-eye, you can still use the Conference Summary Form. Just make sure that you thoroughly document both opinions, state that there are two differing opinions, and then both sign the form. After the parents leave, it may also help to recount the meeting to another colleague if one was not present, or at least take some additional, private notes and give yourself time to calm down and recharge.

☑ Aftermath of a difficult conference

Most importantly, as hard as it is, try not to take the situation personally. It may certainly feel like a personal attack, but often the anger that has been unloaded on you is not truly directed at you. Listening carefully can sometimes give you an understanding of the real problem and help you put the situation into perspective. By taking steps to prevent such encounters, you can be confident that you are doing all you need to do. Any confrontational meeting with a parent should be brought immediately to your principal's attention. Your principal may want to set up a future conference or be otherwise involved in the situation. Document directives from your principal, along with any further actions.

Finally, maintain a good relationship with the student if at all possible. His parent's behavior is probably not under his control. Also, don't change your expectations and procedures just to avoid future contact with the hostile parent. In the long run, it will undermine your ability to effectively run your classroom.

☑ **A Note about conferences and confidentiality**

When conferencing with parents, they may disclose information that they request remain confidential. When discussing certain issues (abuse, divorce or separation, disability, emotional disturbance, etc.), it is recommended that you refer the parents to counselors or other professionals who would be helpful to the child and family. Ask the parents if they feel it is appropriate to disclose the information privately with other teachers or staff members who share the child's day. As a teacher, you are obligated to maintain a level of professionalism whether parents request confidentiality or not. This means refraining from discussing children and their progress, or revealing information disclosed from parents to other staff members who are not in a position to need that information.

Parents should know that the information they share with you is going to be a matter of record, so that there can be no question later about whether you have violated confidentiality. Even if there are no areas of concern, it is your responsibility to verbalize the school policy to the parents if you are required to share conference summaries with the administration, or if you are required to refer cases which require intervention to the principal or social services. Such cases might involve abuse, neglect, or situations in which the child needs additional screening for mental, emotional, or physical problems beyond that which the school can provide.

Summary of Reproducibles in This Chapter

☑ **Pre-Conference/Open House Parent Survey** (page 19) Make your planning easier by getting parent feedback. Send out these forms with the General Conference/Open House Invitation (page 21) so parents can shape the meetings. A separate, Beginning-of-the-Year Open House Survey for Parents is also included (page 77).

☑ **Pre-Conference/Open House Student Survey** (page 20) Use this form to include students in the conference/open house planning process. Often they have as many questions as their parents, and it is empowering for their teacher to give them the chance to ask. A separate, Beginning-of-the-Year Open House Survey for Students is also included (page 78).

☑ **General Conference/Open House Invitation** (page 21) Make parents and students feel extra special by sending them invitations! This invitation can be used for either a conference or an open house, and should make any recipient feel welcomed into your classroom.

☑ **General Event Confirmation Form** (page 21) Parents can return this cut-apart portion of the General Conference/Open House Invitation form to easily let you know whether or not they are coming to the conference or open house.

☑ **General Conference/Open House Reminder** (page 22) Make sure parents remember their scheduled meetings.

☑ **General Conference/Open House Scheduling Form** (page 23) As you get responses from parents, record them on this form. Use a separate form for each day of conferences, and one for meetings which take place for everyone at one time (so that you will know who is coming).

☑ **Conference Summary Form** (page 24) This form is helpful for gathering your thoughts before, during, and after a conference. If possible, have parents sign the form and provide them with a copy so that you both have a reference for what was discussed.

☑ **Facilitation Checklist: Present Yourself as a Professional!** (page 25) Ensure that you always put your best foot forward with parents. Use this checklist to practice your hosting skills.

☑ **General Teacher Conference/Open House Reflection Form** (page 26) Make sure your next session of conferences or your next open house is the best it can be by reflecting on the sessions you just held.

☑ **Handling a Difficult Conference Checklist** (page 27) Prepare as much as you can for those occasional times when conferences are difficult and unpleasant. By reading over and remembering the steps listed in this form, you will be able to maintain your composure.

Pre-Conference/Open House Parent Survey

To the parents of: ______________________________ Date: __________

Dear Parents,

I am planning an upcoming conference/open house on ______________. Please take a few minutes to complete the following information. This will help me choose a format for the meeting and decide what areas to cover. Please return the form with your child by ______________. Thank you for your help!

Sincerely, ________________________
(Teacher Signature)

1. What would you like to know about your child's academic progress, social skills, behavior in class, etc.? ______________________________

____

____

____

2. What would you like to know about our classroom? ______________________________

____

____

____

3. Please list any other questions or comments you have. ______________________________

____

____

____

Pre-Conference/Open House Student Survey

Dear ______________________________________,   Date: ________________

I am planning a conference or open house soon. This will be a time for your parents (and maybe for you) to come into our classroom and see what our day at school is like. Your parents will see some of the work we have been doing in class. I am very excited about meeting your parents, and I would like your help to plan the visit. Please get your parents' help to answer these questions, and return the form to me by ______________________________. Thank you for your help!

Sincerely, ____________________________
(Teacher Signature)

1. What schoolwork and projects would you like your parents to see? ____________

____

____

____

2. What would you like your parents to know about our classroom? ____________

____

____

____

3. What questions would you like your parents to ask the teacher? ____________

____

____

____

____

You're Invited!

Date: ______________________________

Time: ______________________________

Event: ______________________________

What We Have Planned: ______________________________

____

____

____

____

____

Please sign and return the bottom portion of this form. Thank you!

Sincerely, ______________________________
(Teacher Signature)

- -

Event Confirmation Form

☐ **Yes**, I will be able to attend!

☐ **No**, I will not be able to attend. I would like to schedule a meeting for

______________________________.

Child's Name: ______________________________

Parent's Name: ______________________________

Address: ______________________________

____

Phone: ______________________________

E-mail: ______________________________

Best time/way to contact me: ______________________________

Just a Reminder...

This note is to remind you that you are scheduled to attend a(n) ________________

____

on ______________ at ________________.
(day) (time)

Keep the top portion of this form for your records. Then, sign and return the bottom portion of the form. Thank you!

Sincerely, ____
(Teacher Signature)

- -

I received the reminder!

☐ **Yes**, I will still be able to attend!

☐ **No**, I will not be able to attend. I would like to schedule a meeting for

____.

Child's Name: ____

Parent's Name: ____
(Parent Signature)

Conference/Open House Scheduling Form

Teacher ____

Date ____

Time Scheduled	Attendees for Each Session	Special Notes

Conference Summary Form

Student: ________________________________ **Grade Level** ______

Date: ______________ **Type of Conference:** **Personal** ______
Telephone ______

Attendees: ____

____

The following information was shared with parents:

Behavior

_____ Consistently well-behaved
_____ Improved classroom behavior
_____ Unacceptable classroom behavior
_____ Well-mannered
_____ Fine social skills
_____ Sets good example for others

Effort

_____ Hard worker
_____ Motivated learner
_____ Displays sense of responsibility
_____ Follows directions
_____ Does not follow directions
_____ Needs to improve participation
_____ Rushes through assignments
_____ Listening skills need improvement
_____ Poor effort
_____ Poor attitude toward learning

Organization

_____ Uses time effectively
_____ Organized
_____ Disorganized
_____ Lacking the following materials:
____
____

Academic Performance

_____ Standardized test results
_____ Report card information
_____ Improved academic performance
_____ Study skills need improvement
_____ Incomplete or missing homework
_____ Incomplete or missing makeup work
_____ Absences hindering progress
_____ Poor/failing quiz/test scores

Other

_____ ______________________
_____ ______________________

Strategies for Improvement:

_____ Implement contract
_____ Continue current contract
_____ Parent/Teacher to check assignments
_____ Provide a consistent place and time to study
_____ Must improve organization
_____ Must complete work on time
_____ Replace the following supplies: ________
____
_____ Have the student write a plan or strategy to improve
_____ Follow-up meeting on Date/Time: _____
_____ Will provide practice at home
_____ Other: ______________________
____
____
____

Teacher Comments: ______________________

____
____
____
____
____
____
____

Parent Comments: ______________________

____
____
____
____
____
____
____

____
(Student Signature)

____
(Teacher Signature)

____
(Parent Signature)

Facilitation Checklist: Present Yourself as a Professional!

Do...

_____ Survey parents and students
_____ Set a purpose for the conference
_____ Choose a format
_____ Prepare students for information to be shared
_____ Prepare parents for information to be shared
_____ Clean your classroom
_____ Shake hands and make eye contact
_____ Provide adult-sized table and chairs
_____ Display student work
_____ Have pertinent information handy
_____ Have materials organized
_____ Have tissues available
_____ Consider providing light refreshments
_____ Create an inviting atmosphere
_____ Prepare a waiting area
_____ Send home friendly invitations
_____ Send reminders prior to the meeting
_____ Complete summary forms in advance
_____ Dress professionally
_____ Freshen up often to look your best
_____ Greet guests at the door
_____ Introduce all involved in the meeting
_____ Document discussion highlights
_____ Use your best manners
_____ "Sandwich" critical comments between positive ones
_____ Adhere to your schedule
_____ Answer parents honestly
_____ Use sensitivity and tact
_____ Find answers and provide information for parents at a later date if necessary
_____ Meet with struggling students' parents
_____ Meet with successful students' parents
_____ Provide helpful strategies parents can use at home
_____ Allow time for parents to raise concerns and ask questions
_____ Thank parents for coming
_____ Evaluate your meeting
_____ Follow up with a note or phone call

Don't...

_____ Run late
_____ Appear nervous
_____ Dress too casually
_____ Sit behind a desk
_____ Rush through information
_____ "Wing it"
_____ Shuffle through papers
_____ Discuss other students
_____ Make negative comments about colleagues
_____ Hold an impromptu conference
_____ Laugh at students' progress or actions
_____ Criticize parents or students
_____ Agree to anything you won't or can't follow through with
_____ Appear negative toward school
_____ Argue with parents
_____ Appear uninterested or distracted
_____ Communicate only weaknesses
_____ Eat or drink during the conference
_____ Point your finger
_____ Use slang or jargon

Notes

____
____
____
____
____
____
____
____
____
____
____
____
____
____
____
____

Teacher Conference/Open House Reflection Form

Meeting Type: ______________________________ Date: ______________

Give yourself a score of 1-5, with 5 being the best and 1 being the worst.

1. The schedule worked well, accommodated everyone, and provided enough time for all parents and students.
   1 2 3 4 5

2. I was well-prepared to meet with parents.
   1 2 3 4 5

3. Parents learned enough information about their child/the classroom/the school.
   1 2 3 4 5

4. The children who participated were well-prepared and learned from the experience.
   1 2 3 4 5

5. I remained calm and professional in every situation.
   1 2 3 4 5

6. I met my goals for the meeting(s).
   1 2 3 4 5

7. I enjoyed the meeting(s), and feel that others did, too.
   1 2 3 4 5

Notes

Handling a Difficult Conference Checklist

Try to monitor your behavior during the confrontation, and don't lose your head!

_____ Stay calm—your manner will help de-escalate the situation rather than add fuel to the fire.
_____ Remain confident.
_____ Keep your voice firm and level. Take deep breaths and long pauses if necessary.
_____ Say, "I can see you are angry and upset. I want to hear what you have to say, but I need some facts so that I know what happened. Let's have a seat and talk this through."
_____ Take good notes about what the parent says. List problems and concerns.
_____ If you can't meet when the parent is there, schedule a meeting time. Give yourself enough time before the next meeting to get necessary information or to invite another teacher to attend.
_____ Emphasize the importance of working together for the best interest of the child.
_____ Listen! Remember to treat the parents as you would like to be treated.
_____ Don't assume parents don't know what they are talking about or that they don't care. Often parents are concerned but are too frustrated to stop and think about expressing themselves more appropriately.
_____ Parents need to be heard. Allow them to finish thoughts, then pause before responding.
_____ Instead of arguing, ask parents what they think should be done. This assures them that you are listening and care about what they think.
_____ Ask questions to clarify their concerns. Do they have all the facts? Do you?
_____ Summarize parent concerns to let them know you listened and understood what they said.
_____ As you listen, try to determine the "real" reason for their anger. Are they angry at the events they are describing, or is the anger a symptom of a larger problem?

Apologize if you or a colleague has made a mistake.

_____ All teachers, even good ones, make mistakes. Be willing to assume responsibility for your actions.
_____ Work out a way to rectify the error if possible.

Develop a plan! Assign responsibilities to each person involved. Keep to a deadline by setting a follow-up date when you can meet and discuss how well the plan is working.

_____ Agree on ways to communicate more clearly in the future.
_____ Target behaviors that need to change. Brainstorm strategies that will be used at home and school.
_____ Develop a daily behavior checklist, or use an assignment notebook if necessary.
_____ Agree on a date, time, and location for the next meeting to discuss the outcome of the plan.
_____ Include the student at the end of the conference to let her know what the adults have decided and to explain the student's responsibilities in the plan.
_____ End the meeting on a positive note by summarizing the meeting and the plan, and then making an encouraging comment.
_____ Give the parents and child a copy of the plan which all of you have signed.

If all else fails...

_____ Tell parents you must end the meeting if they continue to yell or use inappropriate language. Say, "I am sorry that you are upset and am willing to listen to what you have to say. If you continue to yell, I will have to end the meeting and we can reschedule at another time." Then, do just that.
_____ If a parent threatens you or harms you in any physical way, call the police and file a report.
_____ Move the conference to a location near other staff members or the principal, so that they can see and hear or even monitor the conference.
_____ Be sure to provide your principal with a detailed report of the event and a copy of your notes.

Traditional Conferences

Traditional conferences commonly involve a teacher sitting down one-on-one with parents and discussing a child's academic, behavioral, emotional, and/or social progress. Traditional conferences are frequently scheduled by the school to occur one or more times during the year. All aspects of a child's school experience may be discussed, including topics ranging from recent report cards to friendships.

Sometimes, it is necessary to arrange conferences with parents about specific issues. If academics or behavior become a problem or dramatically improve for a child, it's a good idea to share that information with parents. Academic performance and/or behavior can be inconsistent throughout the school year, sometimes as a result of changing situations at home (divorce, a death, someone new moving into the home, etc.). By conferencing, the teacher can explain what noticeable change has occurred and what impact it is having on the child's academic, social, and emotional progress. Parents, in turn, can give insight into what the child is experiencing at home. Together, a plan can be made to handle the problem as a team.

It is important to remember that traditional conferences need not only communicate problems. While some situations may require the teacher to deliver difficult information to parents, periodically updating parents about students' academic and social progress, even if there are no significant problems, will help to foster and build parental involvement. Consistent communication is one of the most effective strategies you can use to build a partnership with parents which is geared toward meeting the diverse and changing needs of students. And remember, there is never a bad time to reward a child who consistently does well, and to congratulate the parents on their child's success!

During the Conference

Your classroom is spotless and organized. Student work is in neat, rubber-banded piles. Your waiting area is inviting. Conference Summary Forms, Contracts, and Evaluation Forms are in place. Are you nervous? Probably, because the actual conference is about to begin! Most teachers, whether they are brand new or seasoned veterans, feel excited and a little apprehensive at this time, but that nervous feeling is productive in that it keeps you on your toes. Remember that your goal of having a conference, even one that involves relaying negative information, is to do what is best for each student. Stick to your plan to accomplish that, and make adjustments if necessary. By keeping the following pointers in mind as you proceed through the conference, you will be able to give parents the information they need to contribute to their child's success.

Refer to the General Conference/Open House Guidelines (pages 4-17) to help prepare for your traditional conference.

☑ Establish a rapport with parents

Even during the first few minutes of a conference, there are some steps you can take which will help you and a student's parents see each other as allies. Greet parents at the door with a smile and handshake, and maintain eye contact with them throughout the conference to reassure them that you are listening and acknowledging their input.

☑ Limit your focus

If there are problems, be sure to focus on only one or two main problems, so as not to overwhelm parents. Even though you, the teacher, have noticed or struggled daily with the problem, it may be the first time the parents have heard of it. Conversely, the problem can be new to you, but the parents have heard about it year after year from each of their child's teachers, and may be frustrated with unsuccessful attempts to solve the problem. Therefore, it is important to avoid just stating the problem without offering assistance or a plan of action that involves the teacher, parents, and student.

If there are no problems, make sure that you have a brief list of things parents can do to keep their children on the right track. Be as specific as possible with your suggestions, because parents will still want to know what they can do to continue to help their child.

☑ **The sandwich approach**

Begin the conference on a positive note, and end on one as well. By sandwiching negative feedback between praise for the child, you offer encouragement for parents to help their child where needed. As you greet parents, comment on the student's academic strengths or social skills. Discuss the child's interests or hobbies to indicate your knowledge of the child on a personal level. Expressing appreciation of some unique quality or interest of the child's will encourage parents to relax and listen to all of your comments—even the not-so-positive ones.

☑ **Stick to the matter at hand**

As you review each child's academic performance and behavior, stay focused on the child. Do not pass along anecdotes about other students. This can be difficult, because parents may be concerned about their child's interaction with another child in the classroom. However, remember that you will eventually have an opportunity to conference with the parents of the other child as well, so save your information for the appropriate audience—that child's parents!

☑ **Use audience-appropriate language**

Keep your audience in mind. Unless you are talking to parents who happen to be teachers, avoid using jargon. For example, a *basal reader* may mean nothing to parents, so call it a *reading lesson book* instead. Other terms, such as *center*, *portfolio*, *manipulatives*, etc., may also need to be called by other names or at least explained. Stick with language that parents can easily relay back to their children.

☑ **Use specific examples**

Don't speak in generalizations. Comments like, "Lakisha is such a pleasant child," or "Johnny's work habits are poor," or "Celia doesn't get along with others," carry little weight without specific work samples or documented anecdotes. If the comments are positive, parents will certainly want to know more. If the comments are negative, it may sound like you are just picking on a child. Regardless of whether your comments are positive or negative, take advantage of the evidence you have gathered prior to the conference (see pages 11-12) to back up your perspective. Take time to go over the work samples and anecdotes carefully so parents can enjoy their child's successes and identify weaknesses.

☑ Make time for listening

If you followed the suggestions in the *General Conference/Open House Guidelines* section (see pages 4-17), you should have already allotted extra time in your conference schedule for parents to ask questions. If parents seem hesitant about asking questions, involve them in the conversation by asking them open-ended questions about their child's after-school activities, likes and dislikes, or study habits.

Also, speak in positive terms and listen to parents' frustrations, affirming their feelings with phrases such as, "I can understand that…," or "It makes sense to me that you feel…". Even trying to understand how a parent feels will let the parent know that you are concerned and want to help, not blame.

Sometimes it is difficult to get parents to talk comfortably with you. Try to get them to tell you a story about their child. Ask them to explain a funny comment their child made, or tell you their version of a story the child told about an event at home. Or, ask their advice about something you could do that they think will help their child. Knowing you are seeking their input may help break the ice.

☑ Plan to work as a team

Do your best to use parental input to help create strategies for improving their child's problem areas. First, suggest concrete activities or behaviors that parents can use at home. For example, if Darren can't seem to turn in his math homework, suggest that parents sign off on it each night, then watch their child put homework in an assignment folder. If Megan is bullying other children, lend her parents some children's books about bullying to read at home with Megan.

When developing a plan, do not simply plan for action at school. Offer real strategies for parents to help their child at home. Get parents' ideas and incorporate these into a plan as well. Parents may have additional insight about why their child is behaving in a certain way and insight about strategies that have been tried previously. If parents feel you have listened to them and taken their suggestions to heart, they will be more likely to reinforce your strategies at home, creating a united front and more continuity for the child.

☑ Using a contract

Hold yourself, parents, and students to decisions by keeping a written record of agreed-upon strategies. The reproducible **Parent/Student/ Teacher Contract** (page 37) is set up like a frequency chart, and offers a consistent way to measure daily or weekly performance. It can help illustrate to parents and children how often undesirable behavior occurs, and help each child monitor his or her own behavior. The contract can also show a concrete record of improvement by demonstrating that fewer instances of the undesirable behavior are occurring.

If you use a contract with a child, make sure you and the parents set a follow-up date at the time of the first conference. Have some clear goals set, list them on the contract, and plan to meet them by that next conference. Even if the goal is simply to calculate recent spelling grades or to talk to the child about his behavior again, the deadline will help you, the child, and the parents stay focused on the work that needs to be done.

Record any goals or plans of action during the conference on the programmable, reproducible **Parent/Student/Teacher Contract** (pages 37) or on the **Conference Summary Form** (page 24). Get parental signatures (and the child's, if he or she is present), give a copy to parents, and keep one for yourself. If at all possible, word the language carefully so that the child can read it, understand it, and actively carry out the terms of the contract.

☑ **FOLLOW-UP AND THANK YOU**

Finally, after the conference reflect on the meeting by completing a **General Conference/Open House Evaluation** (page 39.) Also, write a note to parents to thank them for meeting with you. Remind them of the goals you set together and include copies of any conference documentation and plan of action. At school, discuss the plan with the student and make sure he understands his responsibilities.

SHOULD THE STUDENT BE PRESENT?

Depending on the age of the child and the focus of the conference, you may wish to allow students to be present during a traditional conference. Parents often enjoy having their children be a part of the conference, and students are proud to hear the teacher make positive comments about them to their parents. Additionally, students are often aware of their own strengths and weaknesses, and can save time by coming up with their own strategies for improvement, pending teacher and parent approval, of course! Encouraging student involvement will emphasize two-way communication. Involving students is an effective way to include everyone and establish a team effort, as well as gain insight about the child's relationship with his family.

You may want to tell students that this will be an opportunity for them to share their own work with their parents. If you make it known early in the year that students will be showing their work to their parents, it may provide incentive to perform even better! If you and the parents are implementing a new plan for academic or behavioral improvement, then it is appropriate to get the child involved after the agreement is made so that the child understands the plan. Look at each situation, student, and purpose for the conference before determining whether to include the student. Refer to the following guidelines to further help you determine if the student should be present.

When determining whether to include the student, ask yourself:
- What is the purpose of the conference?
- What information do you have to share?
- Are you anticipating cooperative parents?
- Are there sensitive issues that might be embarrassing to discuss in front of the child?
- Do you have behavioral concerns to discuss with the parent? Are you hoping to get some feedback or insight regarding that concern?
- Is the conference going to be a negative one?
- Is there a reason NOT to include the student?

It may be appropriate to include the student when:
- The student is doing well academically but would like to establish personal goals.
- The child will benefit by participating in the conference.
- The child's input is needed.
- You and the parents are implementing a new behavioral or academic plan that involves student participation.

Phone Conferences and E-mail

Although face-to-face contact is usually preferred, telephone conferences or e-mail messages may be the only way you can communicate with some busy parents. If this is the case, be sure to document the time, date, and person with whom you have spoken.

- Briefly note the reason for your call or e-mail and the parents' responses. The **Telephone/E-mail Communication Log** (page 38) will help you keep track of parents with whom you have spoken. You can also use the **Conference Summary Form** (page 24) just as you would in a face-to-face conference. Send your signed copy to the parents. If you feel it is necessary, attach a small confirmation note for parents to sign and return stating that they received the note home.
- If you have some parents who can only have telephone conferences, set aside the same time and atmosphere as you would for visiting parents. You may want to even schedule them within the confines of your regular conference schedule, so that these parents feel more involved in the conference process. Also, if possible, call parents from school and not from home, unless you can guarantee that you can have a professional, uninterrupted conversation, complete with textbooks and references to that child's work. Telephone conferences deserve the same planning and respect as face-to-face meetings.
- If you use e-mail, be sure to attach a hard copy of all correspondence to the filled-out Telephone/E-mail Communication Log and Conference Summary Form, and file them in your designated conference filing area.

Talk to parents about the decision to include the student. Remember that it is important to provide the option for a conference without the student if parents feel the need to speak with the teacher privately.

Academic Conferences

Whether a student has consistently had academic problems, is doing just fine, or is in need of extra or accelerated work, you will probably need to hold a conference with parents that focuses on grades and academic performance. Conferences about poor academic performance can be difficult for parents because they know their child is not performing to her potential, and also because parents may feel that your standards are inappropriate for their child. Parents of children who are overachieving in your classroom may be frustrated with what they feel is a lack of appropriate stimulation for their child. It is important, therefore, to make sure that parents understand what you are asking their child to do, and why. If a student's academic problem is severe (either far above grade level or far below grade level), you may suggest testing for special services (see pages 35-36.)

To familiarize parents with how you evaluate students, you may wish to review the curriculum and your behavior, grading, or homework policies with parents, providing them with copies to review with their child at home. If parents know what to look for, they can review work through your eyes before it comes to you for a grade.

If you have parents who need help reviewing their child's homework, provide them with outside academic strategies for helping their child at home. Inform them of tutoring programs, homework hot lines, and other programs that the school offers. Also, copy articles from magazines, the Internet, or pages from professional books with tips for parents. If parents get their child involved in searching for resources, their child will gain a measure of independence in helping himself as well.

Behavior Conferences

Inappropriate and disruptive behavior not only impacts a child's own success at school, but can also impede the learning of his or her classmates. Therefore, behavior needs to be addressed with parents as soon as it becomes a problem. By conferencing with parents, the teacher can share her observations about the child's behavior, discuss its impact on the child and on the classroom, and make plans, together with parents (and possibly the student), for improvement. It is also important to communicate improvements in behavior throughout the year. Parents will feel less anxiety about conferences if they are not always negative. Additionally, positive conferences will not only reinforce the child's improved behavior, but will also reinforce the parents' plan of action.

Before a behavior conference, be sure to check the student's permanent folder to see what behaviors the student displayed in previous years and what actions, if any, were taken. Inquire about the child's behavior with past teachers and with specials teachers. It may help to have other staff join the conference, especially if they are seeing the same inappropriate behavior when the child is with them during the day.

When sharing behavioral progress with parents, remember to use the sandwich technique so that all of your comments about the child are not negative. Also, be careful to avoid characterizing the child as bad or disruptive. It is the behavior that is undesirable, not the child.

Parents may have heard the same behavior concerns over and over, and tried various strategies with little success. Or, this may be the first time they have heard that there is even a problem. Therefore, rather than looking solely to parents for answers, you may want to come up with your own plan of action that will work with your teaching style, then offer ways the parents can support your plan of action. For example, Susie isn't getting along with her classmates. Identify the problem, then offer strategies to help Susie be kind to others. Let the parents know that you will help Susie and list the ways in which you will help her. Then, highlight ways in which they can help reinforce kindness at home.

Once you and parents have agreed that there is a problem, make use of the **Conference Summary Form** (page 24) and the **Parent/Student/ Teacher Contract** (page 37) to set goals and offer specific examples of improvement (or lack thereof). Identify the goals on the Summary and record the behaviors on the contract. Then, arrange a time to meet again and check the progress of the student, so that everyone has an idea of the time frame in which you expect to see improvement.

Although you probably will not have the child present at the initial conference meeting about unacceptable behavior, plan to invite the child if you are using the behavior contract. This way, the child can sign the contract and feel, right from the beginning, that you expect him to be responsible for his own behavior.

Special Needs/IEP Conferences

There are several reasons to modify your conference for special purposes beyond the usual academic and behavioral concerns. Some students may need to be evaluated in order to receive special testing for LD designation, ADHD assistance, counseling, revised placement, or academic acceleration. In most cases, the testing and subsequent evaluations will result in significant changes for the students and the parents. Remember that especially for parents of children who are struggling, special services are a sensitive issue because a child may be labeled as a result of receiving them. Therefore, it is important for you to keep parents involved as much as possible throughout the process. Having a conference before any such change is made will give parents an opportunity to ask questions and discuss concerns.

Traditional Conferences

If you and other staff members decide that a child is in need of testing for special services, be certain that the child will NOT *be present during the initial conference with the parents. This will allow the parents to digest the information and react to it, then prepare for how they would like to react in front of the child.*

IEP *requirements vary from state to state. Make sure you have a good grasp of the* IEP *process, and know where to get more information, before you conference about it with a parent. Remember, parents will have many questions for you to answer!*

An Individualized Education Plan (IEP) is a document used by schools to assist children with disabilities and those who teach them. IEPs are created by teachers, parents, and staff members who work as a team to find more effective ways of educating these children. Before being placed under an IEP, each child must be evaluated according to guidelines which are mandated at the state and national level.

If you feel a child is in need of evaluation, it is wise to first present evidence to your principal and guidance counselor. You will also need to check with your district's requirements about how these decisions are made, who must be involved in making them, and who must be invited to attend the conference. You may wish to have some or all of the additional staff involved in this type of conference. Attendees may include the school principal, counselor, and other teachers who teach the child throughout the day, such as specials teachers. Some school districts offer Intervention Assistance Teams (IATs), and you may want to begin the process of having such a team help with identifying the problem and formulating intervention strategies.

At any meeting involving an Individual Education Plan (IEP), it is very important to walk parents through all of the steps, from the recommendation for testing, to the responsibilities of the different people who will be on the child's IEP team, to the rights and responsibilities of the parents and the child. It is especially important to let parents know what their rights are in order for them to feel some measure of control over their child's education. Finally, make sure that parents have a copy of the plan and that you have their signed consent, in the event of future difficulties. Most importantly, remind parents that part of the IEP process guarantees reevaluation of their child on a regular basis.

Summary of Reproducibles in This Chapter

☑ **Parent/Student/Teacher Contract** (page 37) Let students and parents help you apply this contract to modify student behavior or improve grades.

☑ **Telephone/E-mail Communication Log** (page 38) Keep track of all communication with parents by recording it on this log.

☑ **General Conference/Open House Evaluation** (page 39) Help yourself improve your conferencing skills by asking those who can best help you—the parents of your students!

Parent/Student/Teacher Contract

Goals of this contract:

_______________________'s goal is to ____

____

____

____

Contract Terms:

Each check a student receives will count toward the total goal of _______________ checks.

Actual checks received: _______________________.

Days on which goal was reached:

Week of:	Mon.	Tues.	Wed.	Thur.	Fri.	Comments

Incentives:

If a student meets the goal stated above, then he/she will ____________________________

____

____.

Consequences:

If the student does not meet the goal stated above, then he/she will __________________

____

____.

Contract Accepted by:

Student Signature ____

Teacher Signature ____

Parent Signature ____

 Telephone/E-mail Communication Log 

Student's Full Name ______________________________

Nickname (if any) ________________ Date of Birth ________________

Father's Name ________________	Mother's Name ________________
________________	________________
Address ________________	Address ________________
________________	________________
Phone (Daytime) ________________	Phone (Daytime) ________________
Phone (Evening) ________________	Phone (Evening) ________________
E-mail ________________	E-mail ________________
Fax ________________	Fax ________________
Please circle the best way above to contact you regarding non-emergency information.	Please circle the best way above to contact you regarding non-emergency information.

Date	Form of Communication	Comments	Follow-up

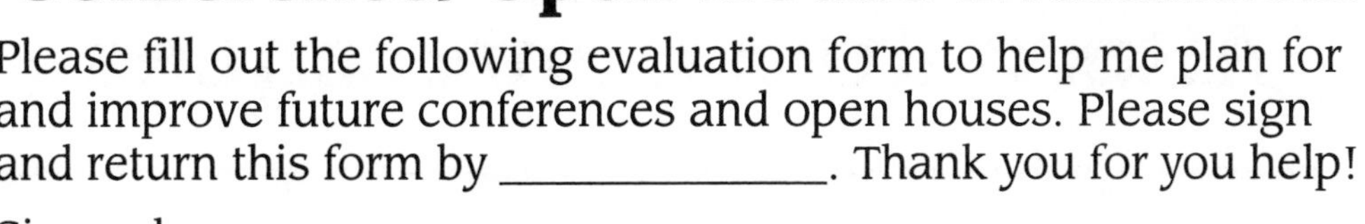

Conference/Open House Evaluation

Please fill out the following evaluation form to help me plan for and improve future conferences and open houses. Please sign and return this form by _____________. Thank you for you help!

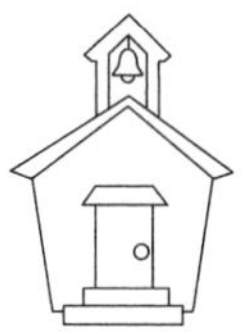

Sincerely,

____

(Teacher Signature)

1. This meeting helped me understand policies and procedures of the classroom.
   very much somewhat a little not at all
2. This meeting helped me better understand the work my child is doing/will do in class.
   very much somewhat a little not at all
3. I am more prepared to help my child at home after this meeting.
   very much somewhat a little not at all
4. (If child attended) My child is better prepared to complete his or her work after this meeting.
   very much somewhat a little not at all
5. My questions and concerns were addressed during this meeting.
   very much somewhat a little not at all
6. I would like to attend another meeting like this.
   very much somewhat a little not at all
7. The length and scheduling of this meeting were satisfactory.
   very much somewhat a little not at all

Please list any additional comments below or on the back of this sheet.

______________________________ ____________

(Parent Signature) (Date)

Alternative Conferences

The previous chapter discussed traditional conferences in which parents and teachers sit down together to talk about a child. Alternative conferences offer less formal ways to share the same information. The purpose of the conference remains the same: to communicate with parents about student progress and performance. However, the way in which this information is shared is different.

Unlike traditional conferences, which are teacher-led and may or may not include students, many alternative conferences are student-directed, allowing students to lead their parents around the classroom, show them examples of work and projects, and tell them directly about their own strengths and weaknesses. This can be accomplished in a small format with one "set" of students and parents, or on a larger scale with parents and students conferencing in shifts. Even though the students present the bulk of the information to the parents, you are still the facilitator of the conference and should be available to troubleshoot and answer questions. You will also still have to perform all of the usual conference preparations and follow-ups, including setting a purpose for the conference, surveying parents, and scheduling conference times (see *General Conference/Open House Guidelines*, pages 4-17).

Student-directed conferences should prove to be a valuable experience for everyone involved. Students will be excited and proud to share with their parents what they're learning, how they're learning, and the insight they've gained into their own abilities and interests. Parents will be especially pleased to attend a conference that allows them to see their children in action. And, you will be pleasantly surprised at the lack of stress (all eyes are NOT on you) and the lack of cancellations!

Individual, Student-led Conferences

While it occasionally may be appropriate for the student to attend a traditional conference, a student-directed conference allows the student to actually lead the conference. An individual, student-led conference is similar in form to a traditional conference. They are scheduled the same, set up the same, cover the same information, etc. The only difference is that the student (not the teacher) gives the information to the parents. The teacher's role here is to facilitate and provide backup for the student if necessary.

☑ Benefits

Student-led conferences can be very powerful. Hearing about school projects, procedures, and progress from the student's point of view can be an excellent learning opportunity for the student, the parent, and the teacher. Conferences are often a mystery to students who fret about what will be said about them. Here, students are the ones telling their parents about themselves, fostering parent/child communication, and turning over ownership of the conference to the students and parents.

☑ Preparation

Preparation for an individual student-led conference will be very similar to a traditional conference (see *General Conference/Open House Guidelines*, pages 4-17, and *Traditional Conferences*, pages 28-36). The main departure will be the need to prepare the student to lead the conference. Refer to the following list of student preparations.

- **Perform a self-evaluation.** Have students use the **Student Self-Evaluation Work Sheet** (page 66) to perform an honest self-evaluation of schoolwork and behavior. You will be surprised to see how well they know their own strengths and weaknesses! As you review their evaluations with them, discuss the issues they bring up and add your own thoughts.
- **Set goals.** Before addressing their parents at the conference, have students establish a plan and set goals for improvement. Use the **Student Goal-Setting Work Sheet** (page 67) to help the student prepare goals for academics, responsibility, behavior, etc., based on the issues from his self-evaluation.
- **Organize a portfolio.** Students will need to gather work samples to present to their parents at the conference. These samples should support their self-evaluations and goals. Refer to *Portfolios* (see page 42) for further information.
- **Rehearse.** Students need to know exactly what to do throughout the conference. Clearly define your expectations of the students' roles, and practice!

Remember to monitor and revise goals throughout the year, and follow up on students' progress with future conferences.

☑ Portfolios

To make the academic part of a student-led conference easier for the student, help students prepare a portfolio of work beforehand. A portfolio is any collection of work meant to show a child's overall capabilities in a particular subject area. Most portfolios are used for writing and language arts, but math, science, social studies, and even art portfolios are equally effective. There are different ways of organizing portfolios. Some contain only the student's best work. Some are arranged to show strengths and weaknesses. Some are compiled to show progress. Another portfolio shows one piece of work through all its incarnations. For example, a portfolio of an essay might show a graphic organizer, first draft, peer review, second draft, edits, and a final copy. No matter which way you and your students choose to organize their portfolios, they should contain enough work samples to clearly represent each child's capabilities. To highlight individual work samples, let each student fill out a **Student Work Sample Evaluation** (page 68) and attach it to any work which is included in the portfolio. By going through what each part of the portfolio represents ahead of time, you and the student will both be comfortable with its content by the time of the conference.

Content Conferences

Content conferences are usually designed around one subject area, and therefore work particularly well for middle school teachers. They can be successful when used at any grade level, and with modifications, can be designed to include all subjects.

Content conferences are another type of student-led conference. They allow students to teach, demonstrate, and practice activities learned in the classroom as they lead their parents through workstations. With some planning and coaching, content conferences can be a snapshot of what goes on in your classroom each day. Unlike an individual, student-led conference, all students and their parents will attend during one session. And, unlike a family night or open house, parents will be able to observe their children's work and discuss their progress. The teacher's role during a content conference is to greet parents, answer questions, and conference briefly with each parent.

☑ Deciding to have a content conference

Before deciding to hold a content conference, think about what is going on in each subject area. Are you completing a special project that has students working on different skills? Is there a content area in which your students will be tested later in the year? Are a number of students showing improvement or lagging behind in a content area? Are parents asking questions about how to help their children in a particular subject? Any of these scenarios could justify a content conference, which will offer an opportunity for parents to see exactly what is happening in that subject area, assess their children's progress in person, and gain confidence in supporting their children at home.

☑ Teacher Preparation

Like any conference, you must plan ahead for content conferences. They are not easy to pull together at the last minute, and will not seem organized without some preparation from both you and the students.

- **Plan your stations.** Choose the different station areas you would like to showcase (refer to the individual subject areas for specific station suggestions), and set them up around the classroom. A **Pre-Conference/Open House Parent Survey** (page 19) can also help you decide what to showcase in each station. Parents may wish to know more about certain skills or activities that their children talk about. Or, have the students suggest a favorite skill or activity that they would like to share with their parents. Refer to pages 45-47 for more information on stations.
- **Set up the classroom.** Before the conference, you will need to clean and tidy the classroom, display student work around the room, and set up the stations, organizing any materials and directions needed.
- **Review student work.** Summarize student progress prior to the conference on the **Conference Summary Form** (page 24), and help students evaluate themselves and prepare their portfolios.
- **Schedule the conference.** Refer to *Scheduling* (below) for more information about scheduling.
- **Send out invitations.** Once you have a workable schedule, fill out and send the **General Conference/Open House Invitations** (page 21). Be sure to state clearly in the invitation that students should arrive with parents and will be conducting most of the conference. You should also send a letter explaining the nature of a content conference and how it will be different from a traditional conference.

*While content conferences do allow parents to talk one-on-one with the teacher, they are not conducive to wholly private conversations. Fill out the **Conference Summary Form** (page 24) as usual, and determine if there are any sensitive issues that may require a separate, private conference. It is best to conduct these private conferences in advance to avoid conflict or embarrassment during the content conference.*

☑ Scheduling

To help schedule the conference, go through the stations with a few student "guinea pigs" and see how long it takes to get through each station. When you are scheduling your conference, stagger time slots so that appointments overlap, but never plan to have more families in your room than you have stations. Keep in mind that there does not have to be a defined beginning station. For example, at the beginning of the evening, you may allow four or five families to start at once. Each family can begin at a different station and continue by following the circuit. It is recommended to cycle through five to six families per half hour. Inviting a guest every five minutes throughout the evening enables every member of the class to have the opportunity to visit each station for 5-10 minutes, and will allow the teacher to speak briefly with each parent in attendance. Use the **Station Planning Checklist** (page 69) to help you plan for work flow throughout the conference.

☑ **Student preparation**

Students also need to be prepared for their roles in the conference. If this is not the first alternative conference you have done, it would be helpful to show a video of a past year's session. Also, prepare students for the event by inviting another class to act as the parents in a trial run. Your students will enjoy teaching the other class about what they are learning and will get good practice for the real conference. To prepare, students should:

- **Organize their portfolios.** Begin your content conference preparation by gathering and organizing work samples in a chronologically ordered portfolio, dating the papers to show progress. Have students use the **Student Work Sample Evaluation** (page 68) to describe and reflect on their work.
- **Make self-evaluations and set goals.** Have students use the **Student Self-Evaluation Work Sheet** (page 66) to gain awareness of weak areas that need improvement and focus on personal strengths. Then, use the **Student Goal-Setting Work Sheet** (page 67) to set goals for improvement based on the self-evaluation.
- **Practice making introductions.** Students must be prepared to introduce their parents to the teacher and vice-versa. Let students choose a partner and rehearse formal introductions.
- **Review the stations.** For the event to run smoothly, it is vital that students are familiar with the five or six station activities chosen for the conference and the order in which they are to progress through them. Review the activities ahead of time and practice reading any directions or explanations at each station. Make sure that students know how to operate any equipment needed and are comfortable with any announcements or text that needs to be read or recited.

☑ **During the conference**

While students and parents are progressing around the room, stopping at available stations, allow them the opportunity to ask you questions. Discuss the **Conference Summary Form** (page 24), prepared in advance for each child, and any notes you've made about how the student is progressing in that particular subject area. Share with parents their children's strengths and weaknesses and areas that need reinforcement at home, and be ready with some suggestions for how they can help. You may wish to be present at the portfolio station (see page 47) to answer questions as students share their self-evaluations and goals. Give the summary form to parents to take home so they can review it and get back to you with any concerns. It is also a good idea to carry a clipboard with you to document any parent questions that you will need extra time to answer. Don't forget to schedule follow-up conferences with parents to address these additional issues.

☑ Setting up stations

Stations are areas in the classroom where parents and students gather during a content conference to look at class projects and individual work, and to complete activities. There are many ways to build your stations, and they will vary greatly depending on your style of teaching, your students' abilities and interests, the type of work or project showcased, classroom space, and the subject area. To make sure you haven't forgotten anything, use the **Station Planning Checklist** (page 69) to help you organize your thoughts for each area. When setting up stations, try to:

- **Offer something for everyone.** Stagger stations throughout the classroom that present a variety of learning techniques and concepts. With a variety of stations, parents will see their children's progress in all areas. It allows every type of learner in your classroom to have an opportunity to shine. For example, if a child is struggling in one area, he can show off his talents in another area at the next station.
- **Use the space you have.** Being able to accommodate several groups of children and parents at the same time is an advantage of conferencing with stations, but a small classroom cannot accommodate large display areas for each station. Be flexible and use the space you have creatively, recognizing that stations can be a bulletin board display, a table with manipulatives set up, a desk with a tape recorder, a computer, a rug and pillows on the floor, chairs set up in front of a television, etc.
- **Stick to what they know.** Now is not the time to introduce new concepts or try new methods. Whatever activities you place at each station should fit your curriculum and be familiar to students due to daily practice. You may want to provide a brief introduction page with the materials so that parents have a clear understanding of the purpose of the activity and how it relates to the curriculum. In writing this introduction, try to use vocabulary consistent with the curriculum and that students will be familiar with.
- **Be organized.** Place written instructions at each station to inform participants of how to complete it. Project boards are effective and inexpensive ways to create attractive displays that include all the information the audience might need. You could also laminate the instructions for durability and simply place them on a table along with all the necessary supplies. If participants will need certain supplies to complete the station, such as a recording sheet, pencils, glue, scissors, etc., make sure these are provided. Parents will also appreciate photocopied take-home instructions on how to use ideas learned at each station so they can practice at home.

Try beginning and ending the conference with purely fun or informational stations. You should begin and end everyones' conferences on a positive note, with all of the areas for improvement sandwiched in between positive comments—the same method recommended for a traditional, teacher-led conference.

☑ **Types of stations**

Below is an overview of the types of stations that can work for a content conference. In the sections dedicated to each individual content conference, there is further elaboration of how to adapt each station to the particular subject matter.

- **Content overview station** This is a good station to put first in the conference because it is a good place to browse. If you have a backlog of parents, they can flip through textbooks, lesson plans, schedules, recaps of field trips, yearlong objectives, etc., while they wait. Also, this station prepares parents for the kinds of material they will be seeing during the conference.
- **Materials station** Parents often have questions about the materials their children use in school and need for particular assignments. If you decide to include this station, demonstrate not only the materials, but how they are used. For example, if students use a particular type of calculator, show the calculator at the station and have each child demonstrate to his parents how to use it.
- **Hands-on station** In this station, the parent and child should do something together. Activities will vary widely with the subject matter of the conference, and can include solving a math brain teaser, reading a book, painting a picture, writing a story, etc. It is appropriate if this station is not practiced by students in advance, so that parents and their children can discover it together.
- **Student teaching station** "See, Mom, you do it like this!" Students will be bursting with pride and confidence when they show their parents how to do something. Have them teach their parents how to solve a math problem, or diagram a sentence, or let children quiz their parents on state capitals of the United States, provinces in Canada, local natural resources, etc.
- **Audio station** Audiotapes have to be executed more carefully because background noise often makes them difficult to interpret. However, taping an interview with a child, a play read aloud by a group, a poetry slam, or any event where parents will easily be able to identify their child speaking are fun for parents to listen to and easy for you to create.
- **Video station** Nothing thrills parents like seeing their children on videotape or hearing their children read aloud. This station can be one of the most effective in your conference, as long as you take the time to teach the children to run the equipment smoothly. Videotapes can be used to show certain activities or skills, but can also be used to show parents what goes on in your classroom.

One way to make a videotape is to have a parent volunteer or student teacher assist you in videotaping children working in centers, playing on the playground (parents always like to know who their children's friends are), socializing in the lunchroom, working in groups, or presenting something to the class (show-and-tell is great fodder for videotape).

- **Multimedia/computer station.** Multimedia presentations are an excellent way to showcase student work. Because using the computer is a skill in itself, you can show parents that students are learning how to use computers while they simultaneously learn the curriculum. Help students use graphic organizers to plan their projects and be sure to allow enough time for the planning and creating process. Also, allow time before the conference for each child to show you exactly how she will execute her project. If you are pressed for time or don't have many software programs, consider quick and easy options, such as letting students show their parents the programs they use (encyclopedia, spelling game, word processor, etc.), an Internet scavenger hunt, or have students type paragraphs about themselves, school, their progress, etc.
- **Portfolio station.** Portfolios are an excellent way to show parents exactly how a child progresses through a project, has shown improvement in a particular area, is struggling with a certain skill, or how well she completes assignments. In this station, students will show their parents their portfolios, work reflections, self-evaluations, and goals. This is an opportunity for students to verbalize their strengths and weaknesses and for parents to respond. This is often a good place for the teacher to linger near, in order to support the student, answer parent questions, and provide additional comments about the student's progress.
- **Take-home station.** Ahh, the end of the line! By now, parents should have a good idea of what their children are learning, and what areas in which they need to improve. So, make sure that parents have the tools to continue to help their children learn. Provide game work sheets, drill work sheets, treats, or a parent information packet that includes different activities or experiments the parents can complete at home with their children. You might also want to include some information about what units you will be studying next and some extension activities that correspond with the material. Don't forget the all-important **Family Evaluation Form** (page 70) to see how everyone liked the conference. To ensure the evaluations get used, place them in a large, well-labeled basket and provide pencils for parents to fill them out on the spot!

There are many software programs available that even very young children can use to combine text, sounds, video, and graphics. Your school may also have digital cameras or scanners that can be used to add photos and drawings to presentations or create slide shows. It is a good idea to check with your school's technology expert for how-to's and ideas.

Language Arts Content Conference

A language arts conference provides an opportunity for your students' reading abilities, spelling tests, handwriting samples, published work, poetry, research projects, book reports, etc., to be seen by parents. Because of the profound emphasis in education on fluency in reading and writing, you can rest assured that parents will always be interested in their children's progress in this area, especially if the students are in third grade or below. Reread the general guidelines for each type of station (see pages 46-47), then try these, or make up your own specific ideas geared toward a language arts content conference.

☑ Language arts: overview of content station

In this station, be sure to flag the materials, explaining them to parents and showing parents what their children have completed. Materials should include:

- anthologies
- workbooks
- grammar textbooks
- spelling textbooks or lists
- leveled reading books
- copies of trade books and other supplemental reading students are using in class
- the overall plan for the year or pacing guide
- state and national standards

☑ Language arts: materials station

There aren't as many exciting materials for language arts as there are for other subjects like science and math, but consider displaying some of the following materials.

- student dictionaries
- writing paper [sloppy copy and final copy paper]
- erasable pens
- writers' checklists
- editors' marks and checklists
- charts with writing or grammar information
- word walls
- big books
- pocket charts and word cards
- sentence strips
- word pointers
- letter tiles
- journals or idea notebooks
- manipulatives (lacing cards, letter tiles, sequence cards, etc.)
- graphic organizers (Venn diagram, story map, story web, etc.)

☑ **Language arts: hands-on station**

It may be difficult to have hands-on activities here. The noise level in the room may prevent reading aloud, and if you have children reading aloud as the focus of your audio station, you may not wish to duplicate it. Instead, try one of these interactive ideas.

- Provide a simple passage with illustrations, along with a work sheet containing guided reading exercises (prereading questions, prediction questions, etc.) to show parents how to use these exercises at home with their children.
- Have parents and children write a few sentences about the conference (what the child did to help prepare, whether the child likes coming to the conference and why, etc.) or about his parents (their names, jobs, etc.) on construction paper and then leave them at the station to be combined into a class book for later reading.
- Provide blank books and let parents and students write and illustrate their own creative stories. To make the blank books, fold and staple several pages of paper together or bind with a binding machine.
- Copy pages of silly fill-in-the-blank stories and have children ask their parents to provide missing nouns, verbs, adjectives, etc., and then read them together.
- Provide a topic, a work of art, or a piece of music for parents and students to reflect on. Then, have them write a poem together, using a specified form, such as tanka, cinquain, or haiku.

☑ **Language arts: student teaching station**

This is the perfect place for parents to be quizzed by their children!

- Let each child give her parents a spelling test. (Determine and list the words beforehand.)
- Have students choose their favorite poetry form and teach it to their parents.
- Students can show parents how to complete a story map, story web, or Venn diagram.
- Students can teach parents how to peer edit using editor's marks.
- Encourage students to teach their parents a song, game, or other activity that is completed frequently in language arts class.

☑ **Language arts: audio station**

Periodically, have students turn on the audiotape and read into the recorder, saying their names and the date, and reading several pages with expression. Have them do this each week prior to the conference. Parents can listen with headphones at the station, reflect on their child's oral reading, and hopefully hear the improvements made throughout the year and pick up on the weaknesses.

Ask parents to donate a cassette tape for their child at the beginning of the year.

☑ LANGUAGE ARTS: VIDEO STATION

Be sure to videotape students' language arts performances during the year to show parents during an open house or a content conference. The following is a list of what works well documented on video.

- puppet shows
- speeches
- group projects
- plays
- library research
- spelling bees
- poetry recitals
- typical language arts class
- dramatic readings
- peer editing and reviews
- tutoring/sharing with another class
- recitations

☑ LANGUAGE ARTS: MULTIMEDIA/COMPUTER STATION

This station can be as simple or as complex as you desire. Simply let students show their parents around on the computer, or let them create multimedia presentations.

Be sure students are very familiar with any software being used during the conference, and know where to find folders, text, graphics, etc., they will need for their presentations.

- Let students show their parents how to use any language arts software, such as spelling games or reading comprehension programs, that they use in class.
- Students can show off their knowledge of word processing programs by opening a page of text, changing the fonts, moving text, adding graphics, etc., to make it graphically appealing. Students can also demonstrate their abilities to pick out the main idea, make it the title, and place the details in a bulleted list. You may wish to provide a sheet of instructions for the activity.
- Showcase students' writing and typing skills in an "e-portfolio." Gather each child's typed work into separate folders on the computer's desktop. At the conference, instruct parents to click on their child's folder to view her work.
- Help students create multimedia presentations for book reports, autobiographies, character trait portraits, research reports, etc. Students can use graphic organizers to plan their presentations and then create a slide show. Each "slide" can give organized information. Student can add text, scanned photos and drawings, voice recordings, etc., to enhance the presentation. Be sure to allow plenty of planning and work time before the conference date.
- Demonstrate letter writing skills with e-mail pen pals. Assign students pen pals (from a different grade or different school) and let them communicate at designated times through e-mail. Make sure that all participants know ahead of time that their mail will be available to parents at the conference. Encourage students to use correct friendly letter form. Let each child access his e-mail folder during the conference to share with parents.

Multimedia presentations can be videotaped and sent home to parents who are unable to attend.

☑ Language arts: portfolio station

Language arts portfolios can be used to easily demonstrate the many kinds of writing, reading, grammar, and spelling work students will complete throughout the school year. Refer to the list below for ideas on what to include in a language arts portfolio.

- book reports
- handwriting samples
- journals
- reading activities
- written compositions
- poetry
- phonics practice work
- friendly letters
- reading tests
- spelling tests
- phonics tests
- "published" work (drafts and rubric) with scoring sheets attached

It is also a good idea to allow students time throughout the year to reflect on their language arts projects. Have students fill out a questionnaire ahead of time which answers questions such as: Which projects were their favorites and why? What are some ways to improve their writing or spelling? What are consistent strengths and weaknesses they see in their writing and language arts skills? If desired, let students use the **Student Work Sample Evaluation** (page 68) to help them organize their thoughts. Place completed questionnaires inside the portfolios for parents to review with their children.

You may wish to place the portfolio station near the end of the circuit because parents will want to read through their children's writing and may take longer at this station than at others. Since the only remaining station is the take-home station, both of these can be self-paced without holding up the remaining parents and children. Parents can find their child's portfolio at the station, then find a place in the classroom to review the materials with their child.

☑ Language arts: take-home station

Take-home stations for language arts can be simple or elaborate, depending on your time constraints and your budget. Here are some suggestions to get you started.

- reading lists of high-interest, grade-level books
- list of Web sites or software packages that are language arts oriented
- copies of a video of an in-class play performance or poetry reading (Include sign-up sheets if parents must share copies.)
- books students can choose from to take home with them, so that a library can begin at home too
- "treat bags" stuffed with pencils, pens, paper, and other fun writing implements for students to practice writing at home

Consider setting up stations centered around topics such as: manipulatives, basic facts review, regrouping, geometry, algebra, computer math, measurement, fractions, estimation, money, time, story problems, graphs, and calculator use.

Math Content Conference

While teachers still have students use paper and pencil activities to practice math, math has moved more toward using hands-on activities (problem solving, manipulatives, computers, etc.). This may be a new way of thinking and learning for many parents. A math content conference allows parents to see these new methods at work, learn ways to assist their children's learning at home, and understand why their children aren't bringing home as many work sheets as in years before. Review the descriptions of content conference stations (see pages 46-47), then choose the topics and activities for each station. Use the suggestions below or use your own best judgment and consider what would most benefit your students and their parents.

☑ Math: overview of content station

At this station, include textbooks and any supplemental materials you use along with descriptions of their use, the curriculum, and what has been covered so far in the year. Materials should include:

- textbooks
- workbooks
- sample work sheets
- sample problem-solving exercises that have been posed to the class
- the overall plan for the year or pacing guide
- state and national standards

☑ Math: materials station

Students now use many math manipulatives that parents may not be familiar with. Be sure to include explanations of use, and maybe even a sample exercise for each manipulative you display. Students can also help parents understand the purpose of the materials. If you are planning any projects that will require special materials, you may wish to post a sign requesting the materials, and include a take-home sheet printed with the items you need to complete the project. Consider displaying the following materials and the teacher's overhead companions to each manipulative.

- calculators
- base ten blocks
- counters
- number tiles
- sorting/patterning items
- rulers
- scales and weights
- math charts and posters
- math journals
- attribute blocks
- geoboards
- tangrams
- protractors and compasses
- fraction bars
- class graphing stations
- play money
- math-related literature
- flash cards and math games

☑ Math: hands-on station

There are many math activities that parents and their children can do together. When planning this activity, try to utilize some manipulatives that parents may not be familiar with.

- Build a "geometry house" or create other pictures from tangrams.
- Solve a problem together, such as *build the tallest tower you can with 9 toothpicks and 7 mini marshmallows.*
- Write a math history of your family, including numbers of siblings, birthdays, ages, age differences, number of pets, etc.
- Create a pizza from construction paper for your family, making sure everyone gets an equal number of slices with the kinds of toppings they like. Then, write fractions to describe the pizza.
- Make pattern necklaces from beads, cereal, or colored pasta.
- Make a math game to take home and play together.
- Race to see who can accurately complete a pentamino puzzle, word problem, or graph in the fastest time.

☑ Math: student teaching station

Depending on where your students are in their math studies, you may want to offer several different skills that students can choose from at this station, so that each child can pick something that he is comfortable with and confident about to teach to his parents.

- Let students teach their parents how to use base ten blocks to show regrouping in addition and subtraction.
- Students can show their parents how to use various math equipment, such as calculators, protractors, balances, etc., then quiz them with problems that use that equipment.
- Have students explain the different methods for solving a problem, such as drawing a picture, using manipulatives, working backwards, or making a table.
- Students can teach their parents math tricks learned in school, such as mnemonic devices, using your hands to show the nines multiplication table, or quickly adding multiple-digit numbers in your head by rounding first.

☑ Math: audio station

Students still often perform math drills, and can certainly be recorded reciting their basic facts. Another idea is to have students record themselves as they orally work out the solution to a problem. It is a good representation of a student's progress to hear their problem-solving logic and understanding of a concept spoken aloud.

☑ Math: video station

This station is easy to set up if you have been videotaping students during math activities throughout the year. The following list of ideas are suggestions for math activities you might want to videotape.

- students receiving math awards
- a class math lesson
- a group problem-solving session
- a math competition or contest
- peer tutoring
- students playing a math game
- students working at a math center

☑ Math: Multimedia/computer station

Math and computers are often closely linked because of computation ability. This station provides an opportunity to share with parents the variety of math applications the computer offers students. Try some of the following ideas.

- Let students show their parents how to use any math-related software used in class, such as math fact review games, problem-solving games, graphing programs, and calculator functions.
- Have students and parents use a data and graphing program to create pie, line, and bar graphs from various sets of data.
- Encourage students and parents to experiment with graphics programs and drawing functions in word processing programs to create pictures from various geometric shapes.

☑ Math: portfolio station

Math portfolios can easily be used to show progress through the year. Include some of the following items in students' math portfolios, along with self-evaluations of their math abilities and progress.

- class work
- group projects
- homework
- math journals
- math presentations
- tests and quizzes
- math stories
- workbooks

To avoid spending a lot of money on items for the take-home station, give away homemade paper versions in place of store-bought items.

☑ Math: take-home station

Provide fun and educational items, such as those below, for parents and students to take home and use together.

- Math fun sheets, such as color-by-number
- A list of simple but fun math activities to do at home, such as recording all the times math is used in a day spent together, or listing all the places numbers are found in their homes
- Math manipulatives such as rulers, shape stencils, tangram sets, dominoes, flash cards, etc.

Science Content Conference

The focus of today's science curriculum has become increasingly hands-on, and students are expected to be able to express what is happening and why in a scientific investigation. Often, parents are ill-equipped to help their children in the area of science because they are not clear themselves about the scientific method, science processes, and even science content. A science content conference is one way to encourage children to express their findings and get excited about science, as well as communicate to parents exactly what kinds of things students are learning about science. Refer to the general guidelines for each type of content conference station (see pages 46-47), and then use the suggestions below or use your own ideas to design the stations.

It is important to determine the purpose of your science content conference when preparing the activities. Activities could reflect major areas of the curriculum, such as earth science or life science, or they could be more specific to your current areas of study, such as layers of the earth, or life cycles. General science topics can also be featured, such as using the scientific method, or using the science processes.

☑ Science: overview of content station

Depending on your curriculum, you may need to showcase several branches of science (physical science, life science, physics, etc.) or just one. Along with the listed materials below, you may wish to include a handout or poster which describes each branch of science and the topics included in each one that will be studied throughout the year. Materials should include:

- textbooks
- sample tests
- experiments that students have or will complete
- list of field trips or major class projects for the year
- the overall plan for the year or pacing guide
- state and national standards

☑ Science: materials station

In a science content conference, this can be a fun station and an impressive display. It is also a good place to request any materials you need donated by parents. Be sure to show a sample of each item you need. It is also fun to lay out all of the materials on a table, provide a list of the names of each item, and then challenge parents and students to match the name to the object. Be sure to provide an answer key and a description of what each item is used for.

- test tubes
- Bunsen burners
- Erlenmeyer flasks
- beakers
- harmless chemicals
- scales and weights
- magnifying glasses
- droppers
- microscope
- human body model
- science journals
- science-related literature
- science charts and posters
- handout with scientific method
- magnet kits
- thermometers
- aquariums, plants, insect houses
- mineral identification chart
- experiment kits
- handout with scientific processes

Alternative Conferences

Activities should be able to be executed in a fairly short amount of time. Determine if your activities are designed to be demonstrations, experiments, or observations and make sure that the students are aware of the difference. Certainly for the student teaching station, you will also want to choose activities that students have experienced firsthand.

☑ SCIENCE: HANDS-ON STATION

It is easy to devise a simple science experiment or demonstration that parents and children can do together. Make sure to provide the necessary materials, such as gloves, water, lab coats, safety glasses, etc. Have a laminated step-by-step instruction sheet available, emphasizing the scientific method and explaining the science behind the experiment or demonstration. Also, make sure you have cleanup supplies handy.

- Use litmus paper or goldenrod paper to test various substances to determine if they are acids or bases.
- Use a mineral identification chart to classify a variety of rocks.
- Use clay to create a model of the earth's layers.
- Make leaf rubbings and sort by size, shape, vein pattern, etc.
- Observe mold samples through a microscope and write a detailed lab report about your observations.
- Blow on a sheet of paper to demonstrate the Bernoulli principle.
- Experiment with magnets to determine the magnetic properties of different objects.
- Use an assortment of materials to represent the difference between a mixture and a solution.

Instead of test tubes, which are time-consuming to clean, consider using disposable, clear-plastic cups or recyclable soda bottles with lids.

☑ SCIENCE: STUDENT TEACHING STATION

This is a perfect place for each child to show his parents an amazing experiment he has performed in the past, has perfected, and is comfortable doing. Make sure that it is a simple experiment or demonstration, and provide enough materials for everyone. Prepare very clear directions for students and parents, including exact measurements, so that you do not run out of materials. After completing the activity, encourage students to explain the science behind the demonstration to their parents, and clean up the station for the next group. Rehearse the following activities ahead of time, or use experiments that students have completed already in class.

- Keep a tissue dry inside a glass even though the glass is submerged in water. (Hold the glass straight, trapping air to protect the tissue.)
- Pick up a pile of paper scraps without using your hands. (Use a balloon charged with static electricity instead.)
- Blow up a balloon without using a pump or your own air. (Place the balloon over the mouth of a bottle as baking soda and vinegar react together inside.)
- Create a substance that flows like a liquid but is hard to stir. (Use starch to make a colloid.)
- Make an apple taste like a potato. (Hold your nose while tasting both a piece of raw potato and a slice of apple.)
- Break a pencil without applying any force. (Place the pencil in a glass of water and observe it from the side.)

☑ Science: audio station

Often scientists record thoughts and sounds on tape to document their work. Let students do the same, creating an audio nature log or documenting scientific observations during an experiment. Each child can have his own tape and start each audio journal entry with the date and circumstances of the recording. At the conference, parents can find their child's tape and listen to it with headphones at a listening center. Another option is to have students take audio tests. Give students a question or concept to explain, and let them speak their answers into the tape recorder. The teacher can record the child's grade and an explanation of the grade on the tape after the child's response.

Audio and video allow parents to learn, firsthand, about their child's understanding of science concepts.

☑ Science: video station

Any science field trip, outdoor project, or experiment is a great opportunity to videotape your class. Try taping your student scientists during the following activities.

- planting a class garden
- on a field trip to the zoo, botanical garden, or science museum
- during a typical science class
- conducting an experiment
- exploring at a science center
- exhibiting at a science fair
- discussing a hypothesis in a small group

☑ Science: multimedia/computer station

This station can be related to the activities in the other stations (for example, lab reports or science logs from the various experiments), or it can be independent. Use the following ideas or work with students to develop your own multimedia projects.

- Students can type their lab reports on the computer and add scanned observation drawings or audio clips.
- Let parents and students go on an Internet science scavenger hunt, finding pictures and answers to questions related to the science topics covered at the conference.
- Help students create a slide show of digital photos of the class conducting an experiment.
- Create a presentation with text, graphics, and sound to explain to parents the steps in the scientific method.
- Have students describe and compare the life cycles of a frog, a butterfly, and a plant using text and graphics.
- Let students use the Internet to get a weather forecast, then use a digital video camera to record their parents giving a weather report. Have them save their movies on the computer.

☑ SCIENCE: PORTFOLIO STATION

You may wish to construct a science portfolio in one of two ways. The portfolio may consist of one long experiment, from idea to research to hypothesis to experiment to results, including photographs of each step, if possible. Or, you may wish to include all of the experiments and activities completed up to that point. Depending on whether you want parents to see grade progression or topic progression, sort the lab work sheets chronologically or by topic. The following items may be included in a science portfolio.

- lab sheets
- lab group assessments
- raw data
- science tests
- class work
- science journals
- self-assessments
- charts, tables, graphs
- research reports
- homework

☑ SCIENCE: TAKE-HOME STATION

Don't forget to offer a **Family Evaluation Form** *(page 70) for parents to fill out at the take-home station. Encourage parents to comment on the effectiveness and their enjoyment of the conference.*

There are dozens of fun experiments students can do at home with their parents. Consider sending home some simple science experiments in resealable plastic bags, such as simple iodine starch tests using foods from their dinners, or offer some of these other giveaways.

- materials and directions to make a science toy
- goldenrod paper
- a magnifying glass
- a list of everyday science experiments
- pH strips
- a bug box
- magnets
- a special rock
- a list of fun and simple science moments to share

Social Studies Content Conference

With the popularity of character education and the rich diversity of today's student populations, your classes experience social studies lessons on a daily basis. Combine these real-life educational opportunities with the traditional lessons in history, culture, and geography, and you have a very good reason to have, and a lot of material for, a social studies content conference. Stations for a social studies content conference can center around a particular region or country, or around a time period or event that your students have studied, showing the many aspects of a culture or time period. Or, the stations can cover the many disciplines of social studies: history, anthropology, psychology, sociology, geography, political science, and economics. Review the general guidelines for content conference stations (see pages 46-47), and then combine the ideas below with your own needs to choose your station activities.

☑ Social Studies: overview of content station

Social studies encompasses many different areas of learning, so it is important to make sure parents know exactly what is considered social studies content for your class. Place appropriate emphasis on what is covered at the current grade level by including the following items.

- textbooks
- sample tests
- project sheets for each of the year's projects
- list of social studies-related field trips for the year
- the overall plan for the year or pacing guide
- state and national standards

Because social studies curricula are often planned across grade levels, it is not a bad idea to post the standard course of study for all the grade levels in your school, so that parents get a picture of what students will cover over the years.

☑ Social Studies: materials station

Although social studies may not lend itself to a materials station as easily as math or science, there are certainly items you can display. Consider including the following items and be as creative as you can, so parents and students alike will enjoy visiting this station.

- wall maps
- globe
- atlas
- topographical map
- flags
- notebooks
- travel brochures
- tour guides
- time lines
- books of photos from other countries
- social studies-related literature
- nonfiction reference books
- social studies charts and posters
- project folders
- compass
- encyclopedias
- artifacts, cultural art, or instruments
- filmstrips or movies

Make an effort to make the activities at these stations fun for the students and for the parents. Parents will be encouraged to work with their children at home when they see how much fun it is to learn and interact with them.

☑ **SOCIAL STUDIES: HANDS-ON STATION**

Students will enjoy completing a project with their parents at this station. Emphasize skills and materials with which students are familiar, but keep the activity a surprise for the night of the conference. Try tailoring these ideas to match your curriculum.

- Send students and parents on a map scavenger hunt. Provide a list of latitude and longitude coordinates and ask them to write the name of each location.
- Have students and parents follow a simple recipe to prepare an ethnic food from a culture the class is studying.
- Ask the child and his parents to plot a car route (on a road map) to a favorite vacation destination.
- Let students and parents make a time line together of family events.
- Have the students interview their parents about their family histories.
- Provide reference books and challenge students and their parents to fill in a work sheet of state symbols, including the state bird, tree, flower, nickname, and motto.

☑ **SOCIAL STUDIES: STUDENT TEACHING STATION**

Ask yourself what your class has learned about social studies, and then design an activity for this station that allows students to show off their knowledge and teach their parents a thing or two (or at least refresh their memories)! Make sure any reports, visual aids, or other materials students will need are handy at the station.

- Students can show their parents how to use a Venn diagram to compare two countries, states, cultures, etc.
- Have students read reports they have written on famous events or people in history.
- Let students show their parents how to use a compass, and lead them to their desks in the classroom using cardinal directions.
- Set up a trivia game for students to play with their parents. Make sure the questions are all topics students know well, so they can be sure to beat their parents! Or, let the student be the game show host and have his parents compete against each other.

☑ **SOCIAL STUDIES: AUDIO STATION**

While video may be more powerful for documenting social studies activities, there are several options for this station. One idea is to have parents and students listen to any audio cassettes with folk songs or dramatic readings that came with the textbook adoption. Another idea is to record students reading in character, as they reenact a moment in history or read from their textbooks. Students can also be taped reciting the *Pledge of Allegiance*, *Preamble to the Constitution*, etc.

☑ Social studies: video station

There are plenty of opportunities to videotape students engaging in social studies activities. Try some of these ideas or provide social studies videos that students watch in class for parents to watch.

- reenactment of a moment in history
- campaign speeches
- a cultural fair or festival
- student debates
- a mock trial or council meeting
- a mock election
- a class discussion
- students working on a group project

☑ Social studies: multimedia/computer station

On the computer, students can execute many of the projects they do in class. Have students try creating a multimedia presentation for their parents, or simply let them do an activity together at the conference.

- Write a short story of historical fiction, based on an event or person from history.
- Search the Internet for important historical events in the past that happened on the current date, birth dates, anniversaries, etc.
- Use one of the many map programs available on Web search engines, and print out a map of the area where they live, or where their parents lived when they were children.
- Set up a slide show presentation of famous people in history.
- Let students show their parents any social studies software they use, like an encyclopedia on disk or geography games.

☑ Social studies: portfolio station

Although history tests are certainly a necessary part of the portfolio station, you can get creative at this station by including some of the following items. As usual, include a student self-evaluation and teacher evaluations of the student's progress and abilities.

- research reports
- homework
- class work
- test and quizzes
- student-made books on topics like community, historical events, or famous citizens
- individual/group projects

Compiling student work into class books allows parents to compare their child's work with that of others in the class, without seeing another child's grades or portfolios.

☑ Social studies: take-home station

Depending on what you are studying, there are many ways to get parents involved in their children's historical ventures. Provide some of these take-home items along with an evaluation sheet for the evening.

- interview questions about what childhood was like for parents
- a schedule of appropriate social studies television programs
- maps/compass
- historical trade books
- ethnic recipes from a country students are studying
- directions and materials to make a time capsule

Although conference night is a convenient time to interact with parents, it is certainly not the only time that you could do so. You may want to consider these options: alternative open houses, sports days, plays, programs, awards assemblies, arts festivals, or cultural fairs.

If you do not have a classroom of your own, set up an area in the library, gym, or hallway.

Special Subject Content Conferences

Specials teachers and support staff often work behind the scenes with students to develop their creative talents or to provide the extra help students need to be more successful in the regular classroom. Unfortunately, these teachers often do not have an opportunity to showcase the wonderful things that they do for children in physical education, art, music, foreign language, special education, etc.

Take advantage of the fact that parents will be visiting school on conference night, and invite them to stop by your classroom to see the special projects and activities that their children have been involved in. Invite the parents of all of the students you work with, or, to make the evening more manageable, target a specific group of parents. For example, just invite the parents of students who belong to your after-school club, who are in a particular grade level, or who are doing extremely well and seem to have a particular talent. Keep in mind that parents of students who are struggling in other areas, but who excel in a special subject area, will especially enjoy hearing positive feedback.

The station ideas for these subjects will vary greatly according to the nature of the subject area. So, rather than breaking down these areas into content station ideas, ideas are listed only under the subject area. Refer to the general content conference stations overview (see pages 46-47) for ideas on how to display these and your own ideas.

☑ Physical education content conference

Often physical education class is students' favorite time of day. They are able to get up from their desks and run and play. While many valuable skills and habits are learned in physical education, parents often dismiss it as playtime. Use a content conference to show all of the important things children are learning in your class. As with other content conferences, get the students involved in presenting the material and evaluating their strengths and weakness.

- Let students teach their parents how to play a favorite game.
- Set up a station for students to show off and describe to their parents any equipment used in class.
- Parents can learn about their child's (and their own!) abilities by performing exercises that require coordination or endurance skills.
- Provide a portfolio for each child with the results of timed trials and skill tests. Include an assessment of sportsmanship and attitude.
- Arrange a fun activity or competition for all parents and students to participate in together, such as a relay race or a parachute activity.
- Have students name, for their parents, the muscles and bones they use to make different movements.

☑ Art content conference

Art class provides plenty of tangible student products for parents to see and touch. An art content conference tends to be a pleasant experience because art is a personal expression and there are no *wrong* answers. As students evaluate themselves, encourage them to focus on their enjoyment of, and confidence in, their artistic endeavors, rather than on whether they think they are *good* or *bad* artists.

- Turn your classroom into an art museum, with a gallery wall to display pictures and podiums (desks draped with cloth) to display sculpture and other three-dimensional objects.
- Let students demonstrate a new art technique for their parents.
- Help students put together art portfolios, showing a project in stages from start to finish or featuring the student's favorite work.
- If your students do graphic art, allow them to show off their skills at a computer station.
- A materials station can be fun if students and parents can experiment with some of the items.
- Provide paper and pencils or paint and let students and their parents create portraits of each other in different styles, such as cubism, impressionism, or realism.

☑ Music content conference

Parents hear their child sing or practice an instrument at home and may attend school performances, but they probably do not know exactly what their child is doing and learning in music class. Invite parents to the music room on conference night to learn songs, play instruments, and see their children in action. Remember to offer student self-evaluations and teacher evaluations of student behavior, attitudes, and listening skills in music class.

- Set up a video station where parents can watch their children perform in a group or participate in a typical music class.
- Create audio portfolios for each child to demonstrate their individual musical techniques and abilities over time.
- Have students teach their parents the names of various instruments they use in the classroom, and present the instruments at a materials station for parents and students to experiment with.
- Share any music composition software or musical web site the students are using.
- At an audio station, provide a CD player and music the students listen to in class. Let the students play their favorite musical pieces for their parents.
- Allow students to perform a short concert for their parents, either individually, or with other students.

Video is an excellent way to show parents exactly what students do during a typical special class.

Don't forget to post a curriculum guide so parents are aware of all of the skills their children are learning.

☑ **LIBRARY/MEDIA CONTENT CONFERENCE**

Arranging a library content conference invites parents to discover that the library is not just a place to check out books, but is also a classroom where students learn how to use the various parts of a book, learn research skills, and develop a love for reading. Let students guide their parents through the following stations.

- The materials station will truly be the entire media center, so encourage students and parents to browse through the stacks.
- Set up a comfortable reading area where students can read their favorite books to their parents.
- Have students show their parents how to use the card catalog to find a specific book.
- Send parents and students on an Internet or encyclopedia scavenger hunt to show off students' research skills.
- Set up a giveaway table with extra or old books the library does not need, bookmarks, or recommended book lists.

☑ **FOREIGN LANGUAGE CONTENT CONFERENCE**

In foreign language class, students are often learning a language that their parents do not know, and therefore cannot easily help with homework. A foreign language content conference can offer parents the opportunity to learn some techniques for helping their child at home, and learn more about the language and culture their child is studying.

- Set up an audio station where parents can hear their child speaking the language, or listen to the language tapes that students use.
- Help parents get a taste of a country's culture by offering a sampling of ethnic foods from the region the students are studying.
- Have students teach their parents simple foreign words or phrases.
- Ask students to interpret what you say for their parents.
- Arrange a computer presentation or bulletin board display with information about the culture, people, and countries in which the language being studied is spoken.

☑ **COMPUTER LAB CONTENT CONFERENCE**

While a computer station is suggested for all of the other content conferences, a computer content conference can explore more in-depth what students are capable of doing on the computer.

- Let students demonstrate software for their parents.
- Have parents and students take typing tests and compare results.
- Create a portfolio for each child on his or her own disk and allow parents to review their child's computer work on-screen.
- Work with students to create multimedia presentations about their experiences, interests, strengths, and weaknesses in computer class.

Summary of Reproducibles in This Chapter

☑ **Student Self-Evaluation Work Sheet** (page 66) This general evaluation form will help students start talking about themselves in a student-led conference. They are also helpful to distribute throughout the year to gauge students' attitudes and opinions.

☑ **Student Goal-Setting Work Sheet** (page 67) A good companion piece to the Student Self-Evaluation Work Sheet (page 66), students can use this to focus on identifying and improving problem areas.

☑ **Student Work Sample Evaluation** (page 68) Let students use this form to describe and reflect on work samples. Attach a form to each sample and include them in a portfolio for an instant conference conversation-starter.

☑ **Station Planning Checklist** (page 69) Keep your thoughts about stations organized with this simple checklist. You can also use the checklist to plan stations for a family night.

☑ **Family Evaluation Form (page** 70) Include students in the conference evaluations. Send home this evaluation for parents and students to fill out together. Use the feedback as a starting point for your next set of conferences.

Student Self-Evaluation Work Sheet

Name ______________________ **Date** ______________________

Thoughtfully answer the following questions about your work in the area of ______________________.

1. One activity I really enjoy is ______________________

____

2. One area that I think is a strength for me is ______________________

____

____

3. The reason this is a strength for me is ______________________

____

____

4. One area that is difficult for me is ______________________

____

____

5. I think it is difficult for me because ______________________

____

____

6. To improve in this area, I will ______________________

____

____

7. Please share any other thoughts you have about your schoolwork. ______________________

____

____

Student Goal-Setting Work Sheet

Name ______________________ **Date** ______________________

The goals I would like to reach are:

1. ______________________
2. ______________________
3. ______________________

The method I will use to reach each goal is:

1. ______________________
2. ______________________
3. ______________________

The date by which I will reach each goal is:

1. ______________________
2. ______________________
3. ______________________

If I reach my goals, I will reward myself by:

1. ______________________
2. ______________________
3. ______________________

Place a check on each day that you do something to help you meet your goal.

Week of:	Monday	Tuesday	Wednesday	Thursday	Friday

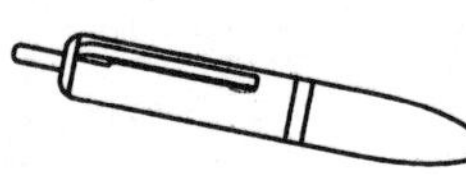

Student Work Sample Evaluation

Name: ______________________ **Date:** ____________

Title of Work Sample: ______________________

1. A good description of the sample is ______________________

____

____

2. The reason I chose this sample is ______________________

____

____

____

3. While working on this piece, I learned ______________________

____

____

____

4. The best thing about this piece is ______________________

____

____

5. If I could change something about this piece, I would ______________________

____

____

Station Planning Checklist

Teacher ______________________________

Date of Conference ______________________________

Name of Station	Purpose of Station	Materials Needed	Time Allotted

Family Evaluation Form

Thank you for our recent conference. Your feedback is important. Please take a moment with your child to answer the following questions so that I can continue to improve my conferences and open houses. Thank you for your help!

Sincerely,

____

(Teacher Signature)

Student Feedback

1. Did you enjoy being part of the conference? Why or why not? ______________________

____

____

2. Do you have a better idea of your strengths and weaknesses in the classroom? __________

____

3. List things you can do to try to improve in the areas you identified as weaknesses. ________

____

____

Parent Feedback

4. Did you enjoy having your child present in the conference? Why or why not? ____________

____

____

5. Do you feel that any goals set are reasonable and realistic? Why or why not? ____________

____

____

6. Do you have any other concerns or questions that we did not address? ________________

____

7. Indicate if you would like to schedule a follow-up conference: ☐ Yes ☐ No

______________________ ______________________ ______________

(Parent Signature) (Student Signature) (Date)

Traditional Open Houses

Open houses are different from conferences because they are NOT designed for parents to get information about their individual child. Open houses are opportunities for parents to see what goes on at school each day, and to experience the atmosphere that their children experience. Parents will not be expecting to talk with you about their children on an in-depth level, although they may certainly use the open house as a time to set up a conference with you.

Traditional, school-wide open houses can occur at any time of day and during any part of the school year. Most school districts schedule an open house at the beginning of each school year to offer parents an opportunity to meet their child's teacher(s), review instructional materials, and learn about procedures and routines. Some districts schedule these meetings later in the school year to showcase student work. Sometimes a schedule is developed to accommodate grade level or classroom presentations, while other times the building is open during the evening for families to visit at their convenience. In both cases, all faculty and staff members are usually expected to participate.

Although most open houses have certain elements in common, requirements will change depending on the type of school in which you teach and the grade levels of your students. As a teacher, you must make yourself aware of your district's and school's expectations and goals for open house. Good sources of information would include mentors, team leaders, department chairs, and building administrators. Often, a format for open house is discussed at an early staff meeting.

Open houses are a great way to share news about classroom activities and children's progress with all parents in an hour or less in an informal atmosphere. You will be able to do this by enlisting the help of your students to greet their parents and share their portfolios, stations, or centers. Parents will enjoy the quality time spent with their children, and your students will love showing and telling all about their work and their classroom.

There are similarities between open houses and content conferences. However, the focus of an open house is the word "open." All displays are for everyone to see at an open house, and the focus should be on the school, classroom, or subject as a whole, not the individual student.

Traditional, Beginning-of-the-Year Open House

A beginning-of-the-year open house is held prior to the opening of school. The primary purpose is to provide a chance for students and parents to meet you, to visit their new classroom, to pick up supply lists, to find their lockers and desks, and to display books and materials. Parents and students will be prepared for the first day, and the stress caused by trying to anticipate the unknown will be relieved for all of you! Students are guests with their parents.

In addition to helping students and parents get acclimated to a new school environment, there is an advantage to having this type of open house for you, the teacher. Scheduling a time for all parents and students to visit your classroom will eliminate the many interruptions caused by drop-in visitors as you are trying to set up your room. It will also give you the opportunity to meet your new students and their parents in a classroom that has been organized and prepared to welcome them to an exciting new year.

Using a survey before your open house will give you an advantage with your new students. You will be able to gauge students' anxieties about school and take steps to confront any issues they have before the first day of class.

☑ Surveying parents and students

Just like in conferences, surveying parents and students, even before school starts, will help you design an open house that is informative for everyone attending. Use the **Beginning-of-the-Year Open House Parent Survey** (page 77) and the **Beginning-of-the-Year Open House Student Survey** (page 78) instead of general surveys. The difference between these forms is that the survey in this chapter does not ask what kinds of work parents and students would like to see. Rather, it focuses on what information they would like to have about the new classroom and teacher. Also, mail the **All About My Child** survey (page 79) to parents before the event and encourage them to bring it to the open house.

Share the results of the survey with parents and let them know how you intend to address their concerns or needs. In many instances, you could do this with a newsletter home or as part of the invitation to your open house. Individual concerns of a personal nature can be handled in a personal note or with a phone call.

☑ Scheduling

Most school-scheduled open houses last 45-60 minutes, although the floating type held by schools in which children have several teachers may last much longer. Even in a floating open house, parents will expect to be greeted, and will probably ask you the same questions over and over. Try to give your opening presentation to small groups as they come in, but anticipate a lot of necessary repetition. Use the **Open House Checklist** (page 80) and the **General Conference/Open House Scheduling Form** (page 23) to help you map out how long it may take you to greet each small group and give them pertinent information (in the form of packets). Once your schedule is set, send out the **General Conference/Open House Invitation** (page 21) to parents.

☑ **PREPARING YOURSELF, YOUR CLASSROOM, AND YOUR MATERIALS**

As the saying goes, you don't have a second chance to make a good first impression. Think about it from the children's and parents' perspective: this is the atmosphere in which students will spend a large portion of each weekday for the next nine months! Open houses are an opportunity for parents to meet you, other teachers, and support staff, as well as to see firsthand the learning environment you have created for their children. They will expect to learn classroom procedures and routines, and to become aware of your expectations and goals for the school year. Attention to detail in your classroom and in the quality of information you give to parents can be well worth the time and effort it takes to create a warm, friendly learning environment, and will do a lot to alleviate the first-day jitters for students. Refer to the *General Conference/Open House Guidelines* (see pages 4-17) and use the **Facilitation Checklist** (page 25) to make sure you are ready for this first meeting with parents and students.

If your open house is "floating," as many are, rehearse a brief introduction of yourself and the material you want parents to see. Greet parents individually or in small groups as they walk in, and let them know what to look for as they move about your classroom. Also, make yourself available for general questions as much as possible.

Parents will be especially interested in what changes they and their children will experience when it comes to grades, policies, and procedures. Children will be interested in these also, but they will want to know other important information, such as class celebration policies, days off, and, of course, where the rest rooms are! At open house night, you may want to provide information about and copies of:

- school handbook highlighting important names and phone numbers
- school calendar
- school or hallway map
- daily/bell schedule
- special class schedules—gym, art, music, etc.
- materials list
- textbook information
- formal testing information
- grading scale
- grade level information
- lunch program
- homework policy
- attendance and makeup work policies
- current fund-raisers
- clubs and organizations
- classroom rules and consequences
- discipline plan
- rewards
- transportation information
- policies regarding parties or birthdays

Remember, parents and students may want to tour the building. If you have a teaching assistant, you may want to make him or her responsible for leading brief building tours. Be sure to show new students where to find the lunch room, gym, lockers, and rest rooms!

Traditional Open Houses

To enhance parents' understanding of materials, as well as the impact of their packets, have a make-it/take-it session during the open house where they can make games and materials to take home and use with their children.

Be prepared and willing to introduce parents to each other. Parents may begin to establish networks with other parents and find volunteer program information that interests them.

☑ Display ideas

Think about including some of the following at your open house.

- Display an "About the School" bulletin board showing photographs of the principal, vice-principal(s), special teachers the children will encounter, and a schedule of special classes.
- Create an *All About Me* bulletin board that is all about...you! Include photographs and text sharing your hobbies, special interests, family, vacations, etc., to introduce children to their new teacher.
- Make a "donations needed" bulletin board by attaching self-adhesive notes with items such as tissues, snacks, pencils, paper, etc., that parents may wish to donate. Or, use the **Volunteers and Supplies Needed!** form (page 81) to ask for donations or encourage volunteers for field trips, guest readers, career sharing, etc.
- Display textbooks, work sheets, and other materials you plan to use in your classroom for parents and students to look at together.
- Put chairs down, turn lights on, decorate bulletin boards, and label desks and lockers.
- Post the **Open House Sign-In Sheet** (page 82) to help you remember who you have met after a night of greeting people.
- Display student job assignments, and even assign jobs ahead of time, if possible. Make sure that students without jobs have their names displayed around the board, and provide a few extra, blank name pieces for children who may attend the open house but did not register in time to make your roster.

☑ Structuring the open house night

Regardless of whether your open house is floating or stationary, parents will expect to be greeted and then directed through any events you have planned. To give this direction, make sure that there is a definite beginning, middle, and end to your open house night. Even if you have to repeat this format several times for a floating open house, parents will feel as if they have gotten all of the necessary information.

- Begin with a short presentation by you, by small groups of students, or with a multimedia program or video (see page 75). In this part, stress the goals of the evening by listing what you would like parents to take home from the open house (literally or figuratively).
- After the presentation, hand out packets (see page 75) and go over the contents. Or, staple a checklist of the contents on the outside of the packet so that parents can make sure they have everything.
- Next, give parents a chance to visit stations or centers that stress the strategies you discussed. Let them see samples of past student work that illustrate the concepts being discussed.
- Wrap up the open house with a question-and-answer period and a chance to fill out evaluations (see page 76).

☑ The multimedia option

One way to add interest and fun to your open house night is to start out the evening with a multimedia format (videotape, audiotape, slide show, etc.) While multimedia presentations are not difficult to create, planning is essential in order to utilize available resources efficiently and communicate your desired message.

- Floating open houses require special consideration because parents will not all attend at the same time. Consider having a looping (repeating) videotape, or a slide show station where parents and students can sit down and view the slides at their own pace.
- At a beginning-of-the-year open house, a looping videotape showing areas of the school and "introducing" staff members will help address visual learners' needs and help them put faces with names.
- Simple slide shows can be created on a computer to inform parents of policies and procedures. Accompanying handouts are helpful if you are presenting a great deal of information or if you need to communicate with parents and students who may not have been able to attend. Many software programs provide options for printing from the slides.
- Depending on the type and purpose of your presentation, you may need to arrange the room differently, arrange for a large monitor and seating area, turn off lights in one part or all of the room, etc. Make sure your room is arranged before the parents arrive and always plan for more parents than you anticipate.

If you wish to have a multimedia presentation showing students in your classroom, you can use your "footage" from the previous year at a beginning-of-the-year open house.

☑ Open house packets

Rather than spending your limited time going over all of this information in detail, provide a packet that parents can take with them for future reference. Use the ideas from page 73, and from any surveys you send out. Any questions about materials in the packet can be answered at a later date. Parents will appreciate having extra time after the open house to go through the information with their children, too, in order to better prepare them for what to expect.

You may want to include some short assignments to be turned in the first day of class. Although you will further assess the academic and social needs of your students, a few "fun" assignments can go a long way in telling you more about your class. Consider sending home:

- basic facts work sheet
- "what I read this summer" work sheet
- "favorites" questionnaire (favorite book, TV program, food, etc.)
- a note card on which students can write their names, names of family members and friends, the alphabet, etc.

☑ **EVALUATIONS**
Be sure to have parents and students fill out a **Beginning-of-the-Year Open House Evaluation Form** (page 83) or a **General Conference/ Open House Evaluation Form** (page 39) as they leave. You will learn a lot about what additional information parents and students would like to have before starting the school year!

TRADITIONAL, MIDDLE-OF-THE-YEAR OPEN HOUSE

A middle-of-the-year open house is usually arranged to showcase students' work and achievements. Portfolios are shared and student performance is highlighted, but it is not a conference because parents are there to learn about class work as a whole, not just as it applies to their child. Let students guide parents through the classroom, acting as experts by explaining centers, class activities, and projects.

Refer to the *General Conference/Open House Guidelines* (see pages 4-17) and to the *Traditional, Beginning-of-the-Year Open House* section (see pages 72-76) for information about planning and executing your open house. The traditional middle-of-the-year open house will be very similar to the beginning-of-the-year open house. The main difference will be that the students, rather than the teacher, will make most of the displays and share most of the information with their parents.

SUMMARY OF REPRODUCIBLES IN THIS CHAPTER

☑ **Beginning-of-the-Year Open House Parent Survey** (page 77) This form is similar to the Pre-Conference/Open House Parent Survey (page 19), but it does not address questions about what work parents would like to see, as there is none yet.

☑ **Beginning-of-the-Year Open House Student Survey** (page 78) Similar to the Pre-Conference/Open House Student Survey (page 20), this form's purpose is to alleviate students' anxiety about the coming school year and new situations.

☑ **All-About-My-Child** (page 79) Have parents bring this form to the open house. You will learn a lot about your new students.

☑ **Open House Checklist** (page 80) This planning page is designed to help you disseminate information about your school and class that new parents and students need to know.

☑ **Volunteers and Supplies Needed!** (page 81) Program this sheet to ask parents to donate supplies, to volunteer to be field trip chaperones, or for anything else parents might be able to help with.

☑ **Open House Sign-In Sheet** (page 82) will help you keep track of who came, and of your "traffic flow."

☑ **Beginning-of-the-Year Open House Evaluation Form** (page 83) Get feedback from parents by having them fill out this form.

Beginning-of-the-Year Open House Parent Survey

To the parents of: ______________________________ Date: __________

Dear Parents,

I am planning for a beginning-of-the-year open house on ______________. Please take a few minutes to complete the following information, then return this form to me. This will help me choose a format for the open house and decide what areas to cover. Please return the form by ______________. Thank you for your help!

Sincerely, ________________________
(Teacher Signature)

1. What would you like to know about our school? ______________________

____

____

2. What would you like to know about our classroom? ______________________

____

____

____

3. Please list any other questions or comments you have: ______________

____

____

____

____

____

Beginning-of-the-Year Open House Student Survey

Dear ____, Date: ____________________

I am planning to have a beginning-of-the-year open house. This will be a time for you and your parents to visit our school and classroom. I am very excited about meeting you and your parents, and I would like your help to plan the visit. Please get your parents' help to answer these questions, and return the form to me by ______________________________. Thank you for your help!

Sincerely, ___________________________
(Teacher Signature)

1. What would you like to know about our school? ______________________________

____

____

2. What would you like to know about our classroom? ______________________________

____

____

____

3. What questions would you like to ask me? ______________________________

____

____

____

____

____

____

All About My Child

Dear Parents,

I would like to know more about your child so that I can better meet his or her individual needs. Please take a moment to complete this get-to-know-you letter and return it to me at the open house or by ____________.

Thank you, ______________________________
(Teacher Signature)

Child's Name ____________________
Parents' Names ____________________
____
____
Phone Number ____________________
Best time to be reached ____________

1. What motivates your child? ______________________________

____

2. What kinds of things upset your child? ______________________________

____

3. List five words that best describe your child's character and/or personality: ____________

____

4. My child's areas of strength are: ______________________________

5. My child struggles with: ______________________________

6. How would you rate your child's attitude toward school? 1 2 3 4 5
Needs Improvement ←——→ Super

7. How would you rate your child's sense of responsibility? 1 2 3 4 5
Needs Improvement ←——→ Super

8. Are there any personal or medical problems of which I should be aware? This information will be shared with the school nurse if medication is involved. ______________________________

____

9. Do you have any additional comments or concerns? ______________________________

____

Thank you for completing this form. I know that together we can make this year successful for your child.

______________________________ ____________
(Parent Signature) (Date)

Open House Checklist

Teacher ______________________________ Date ________________

☐ **Opening Presentation/Comments:** ______________________________

____

____

Time Allotted: ______________________________

☐ **Class/School Policies and Procedures Overview:** ________________

____

____

Time Allotted: ______________________________

☐ **Volunteers/Donations Needed:** ______________________________

____

____

Time Allotted: ______________________________

☐ **Class Projects/Upcoming Work:** ______________________________

____

____

Time Allotted: ______________________________

☐ **Question-and-Answer Session:** ______________________________

Time Allotted: ______________________________

Volunteers and Supplies Needed!

Please sign up if you can help!

We need supplies:

We need volunteers for these events:

We need ____________________:

We need ____________________:

Thank You!

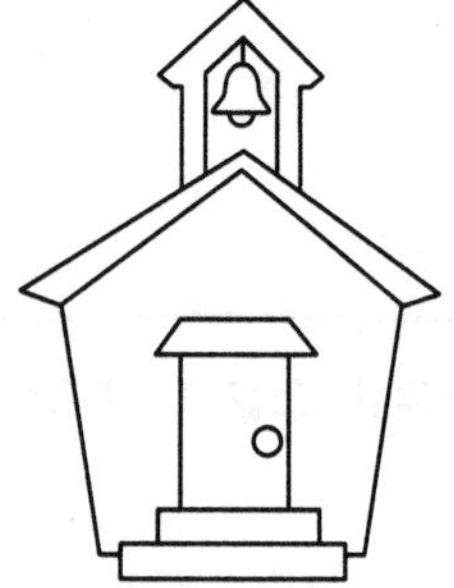

Open House Sign-In Sheet

Dear Parents and Students,

Please take a moment to sign in as you enter the open house. It will help me remember who attended at a later date. Thank you!

Date ____________________ Time ____________________

Names of Open House Attendees	Comments

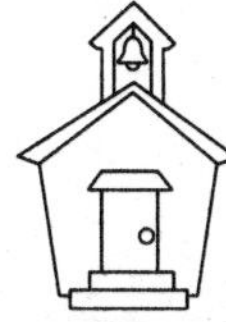

Beginning-of-the-Year Open House Evaluation

Thank you for attending our recent open house. Your feedback is important. Please take a moment with your child to answer the following questions so I can give you any additional information you may need. If you have any other comments or questions, list them on the back of this form. Please return the form by ____________________.

Sincerely,

____
(Teacher Signature)

Student Feedback

1. Were your questions about your new school and/or class answered at the open house?______________

   If not, what additional questions do you have?________________________________

   ____

   ____

2. What are you looking forward to this school year? ____________________________

   ____

3. What do you think will be difficult about this school year? ______________________

   ____

4. What was the most important thing you learned at the open house? ________________

   ____

Parent Feedback

5. Were your questions about your child's new school and/or class answered at the open house?________

   If not, what additional questions do you have?________________________________

   ____

   ____

6. What do you think your child will need extra help with during the school year?______________

   ____

   ____

________________________________ ________________________________ __________
(Parent Signature) (Student Signature) (Date)

Alternative Open Houses

Although the most common type of open house is the introductory one, there are many other reasons to have an open house, such as showcasing students' work, sharing strategies for parents to help their children at home, or providing information about school policies and programs. One advantage to holding an alternative open house is that students, parents, and teachers all have information they need, questions they want answered, and ideas they want to share throughout the school year. Another advantage is that sharing with parents, involving students, and keeping open lines of communication create a strong school community feeling between parents and teachers, and a strong classroom community feeling between students and teachers.

Determine the type of open house that best meets parents', students', and your own needs. The following pages offer ideas for planning several different types of open houses. Try some of the options suggested here, or develop your own unique type of open house. No matter what format you choose, remember to have parents, students (and you!) evaluate the open house so that you can make each year's presentation even better than the last!